BATTERSEA
DOGS' HOME

BATTERSEA
DOGS' HOME

Inside the
World-famous
Home for Dogs
...and Cats

ROBIN McGIBBON AND BOB LONG

BBC

Acknowledgements

Dozens of delightful people at the Dogs' Home deserve thanks for their help in making this book such an interesting and enjoyable one to write. Particular mention, however, must be given to Duncan Green, Shirley Piotrowski, Nichola Vickers and Sarah Ruff, and also to the Home's Committee. Finally, a very sincere thank you to Sue McGibbon for the days spent behind the scenes with staff – many who are not mentioned in this book – and for transcribing and editing the interviews swiftly to ensure we met the tight deadlines.

This book is published to accompany the BBC television series
Battersea Dogs' Home, first broadcast in 1998.
Executive Producer: Bob Long
Series Producer: Steve Sklair
Producer: Sarah Topalian

Published by BBC Worldwide Ltd, Woodlands, 80 Wood Lane, London W12 0TT

First published 1998
© Robin McGibbon and Bob Long 1998
The moral right of the authors has been asserted

Photographs by Emma Louise Ogilvy © BBC 1998

We would also like to thank the following for contributing their photographs:
Jane Barber page 154 and 155; Jane Belasco 127; David Cavill 139 (above);
Maria Crowley 71; Jade Hall 138; Denise McFarland-Cruickshanks 130–131
and 135; Marion Oak 139 (below); Michelle Ritter 125.

ISBN: 0 563 38470 0

Commissioning Editor: Anna Ottewill
Copy Editor: Angie Mackworth-Young
Designer: Jane Coney

Set in Century Old Style by BBC Books
Printed by Cambus Litho Ltd, East Kilbride
Bound by Hunter & Foulis Ltd, Edinburgh
Cover printed by Belmont Press, Northampton

Contents

The lady who started it all

Duncan Green had been Director General of the Dogs' Home Battersea for eight months when his secretary, Shirley Piotrowski, came into his office, looking thrilled.'Great news,' she said, waving a letter in front of him. 'That vicar has confirmed what we thought.' The retired Army Lieutenant Colonel beamed. 'It's there?' 'Yes,' said Shirley. 'We can go there any time we want.' 'You want to, don't you, Shirley?' 'We must, Duncan,' Shirley replied, earnestly. 'We must. We owe it to her.' Duncan nodded. 'Fix a date. We'll go together.' 'We'd better go prepared,' Shirley said. 'It's in a terrible state, I gather.'

At lunchtime, the following Friday, 24 September 1993, the Colonel and Shirley drove out of the Home on to Battersea Park Road, with a bucket, a bottle of bleach, brushes and wirewool in the boot, and a warm feeling of expectancy in their hearts.

They were heading 40 miles north, to perform a duty they felt right and proper, not for themselves, but for a remarkable woman, whose humanity, unquenchable caring spirit and courage had transformed so many lives over the past 133 years.

Battersea's Director General, Duncan Green, in his office with Shirley Piotrowski's Shih Tzu, Mandy.

Moving out of the bustling London traffic on to the free-flowing M1, the mood in Duncan's Saab was as bright as the early autumn sunshine, with the secretary and her boss chatting excitedly about what lay ahead of them in the Bedfordshire town of Biggleswade.

Shirley's morbid fascination with cemeteries had prompted her to play detective, and she had made inquiries at several churches in the town before tracing the one she was looking for. But it was far more than a trivial, passing interest in the secrets that might lie behind the decaying gravestones that was driving them to St Andrews Church today. It was the

A new arrival begins its Battersea life in the kennels bearing Mary Tealby's name.

historical significance and overwhelming relevance to Battersea's glorious past.

Like others before him, Duncan found it astonishing and deeply sad that so little was known of the brave woman who had started the Dogs' Home in a stable yard in Holloway, north London, all those years ago. All he knew was what he had read in a commendable history of the Home, graphically written by Gloria Cottesloe – one of the current Committee members – 20 years before.

He knew that the woman was separated from her husband, a timber merchant from Hull.

He knew she had a brother, Edward Bates, a clergyman, who persuaded his rich and influential friends to support her campaign to rescue dogs in distress.

He knew she had been tough and courageous enough to withstand the ridicule of a scathing Victorian press and build up her dog sanctuary to the point where she was caring for more than 200 animals a week.

And he knew she had lived with her brother in a small house in Islington before she died from cancer, aged 64, in 1865.

But that was all. There was no other information – not even a photograph to show what the remarkable woman looked like. The only tangible relic from her fulfilling life was her signature on the minutes of those early Dogs' Home

Shirley Piotrowski whose detective work traced the last resting place of Mary Tealby.

committee meetings – a signature Duncan Green would look at in some awe as he contemplated the enormity of the woman's success and the difficult times and circumstances in which she achieved it.

Now, however, thanks to *The Biggleswade Chronicle,* and her own perseverance, Shirley Piotrowski had located the great lady's last resting place. Why it was in Biggleswade no one knew, and never would. What was important to Duncan and Shirley was the grave itself, and as they turned into Shortmead Street and stopped outside the vicarage, still chatting excitedly, Duncan and his ebullient secretary couldn't wait to see it.

They got a shock: all the headstones from the graves in the churchyard had been removed and what was once a cemetery had been flattened and turned into a grassy garden of rest. They introduced themselves to the vicar, the Reverend Robert Sibson, who took them to a remote and gloomy corner of the churchyard and pointed to what they had come to see: beneath a large tree, deprived of sunlight and covered in lichen, was a flat, unassuming slab of granite – a horizontal tombstone, with an inscription on either side, confirming that two people were buried there. On one side, it read: 'Reverend Edward Bates, died June 5th 1876, aged 72.' On the other, barely legible through years of neglect, were the words Duncan and Shirley were looking for: 'Mary Tealby, widow, born December 30th 1801. Died October 3rd, 1865.'

They stared at the inscription, feeling a mixture of surprise and disappointment. Then they looked at each other sadly: for someone who had done so much with her life, the desolate grave was a travesty, and the sooner they did something about it, the better.

The vicar offered them the use of a kitchen in the church hall and, for the next two hours, Shirley ferried buckets of water backwards and forwards to the grave, while Duncan scrubbed it clean with wire wool and a brush. Then Shirley walked into the town to buy a flower to plant in Mary's memory. She wanted something feminine for a lady; something colourful to brighten the gloom of that remote corner. She chose a pink chrysanthemum, and Duncan planted it at the foot of the grave, and they stood silently for a few moments, thinking of Mary Tealby, and how much they, and so many others, had to thank her for.

The parishioners of St Andrews were preparing for an open day, and the work on Mary's tombstone attracted a lot of attention. Before leaving, Duncan and Shirley were asked to write something, explaining why the grave, neglected for so long, had been tended so unexpectedly and with such loving care. They got a sheet of plain white paper from the church hall and borrowed a felt-tip pen. Duncan asked Shirley to write some appropriate words and she wrote: 'Mary Tealby, founder of the Dogs' Home, Battersea, in 1860, is buried here.' She handed the paper to the vicar, who said he would make sure it was seen, then she and Duncan said their goodbyes and walked slowly to the car.

They were quiet for most of the journey: they were pleasurably exhausted and felt no desire to talk. It had been an emotional afternoon for both of them and it seemed right to just sit in reflective silence.

Tealby Kennels, the three million pound building that gave thousands of dogs a better chance.

Approaching Battersea, Shirley found herself thinking of the words she had written for those visitors who passed Mary's grave. As an epitaph, they were so insufficient, so understated; and for them to be left on just a sheet of paper beside a slab of granite, in a provincial churchyard, was hardly a fitting tribute to a woman whose vision had initiated the great work that was still flourishing today. What Mary really warranted, Shirley thought, was a more relevant monument, something that symbolized the devotion to dogs that had driven her to make such a lasting impact in Britain.

They drove through the iron gates at the front entrance to the Dog's Home and stopped outside the offices. Unloading the cleaning gear from the boot, Shirley looked to her right, at the long rows of old, ground-level, 4ft by 4ft kennels, where 300 dogs waited to be re-homed, then at the modern building ahead of her.

The four-storey building, which had cost £3 million, had been opened by the Queen two years before, and provided a warmer, more welcoming sanctuary for the thousands of lost or unwanted dogs brought to Battersea every year.

Looking at the building, Shirley suddenly realized that the memorial she felt Mary Tealby so richly deserved was staring her in the face.

It was named Tealby Kennels. And, despite many reservations about its design, Shirley felt it was the ideal monument to Battersea's fearless founder, whose devotion had saved so many starving dogs in Victorian times.

CHAPTER ONE

The strays rescued from the streets

Pauline Martignetti with one of the strays collected from a London police station.

It is seven o'clock on a miserable Monday morning in March. A biting wind has blown an icy chill on to south London's rainswept streets, but the young woman driving the red animal ambulance in just a thin lilac T-shirt is as oblivious to the cold as she is to the wind and rain. The weather bothers her little; the windier and colder the better, for she is what she calls a winter person who would far rather hug a seal in the Antarctic than snooze under a scorching sun. Her name is Pauline Martignetti and what gets her up on dark, dank days like this is the thought of lost or abandoned dogs cowering, lonely, frightened and confused, behind the bars of primitive kennels in places they have never seen before. Pauline, just 4 foot 10 inches, with size 2 feet, is head of four Battersea drivers – one of whom is her husband, Martin – who travel hundreds of miles in London and the surrounding areas within the M25, collecting strays from police stations and taking them to the warmth and security of the Dogs' Home and the caring people who work there.

Ten years ago, the list of stations holding strays was telexed to Battersea police from Scotland Yard and taken to the Dogs' Home by a little old man on a bike. Now, the list is faxed to the Home direct overnight. By 6.45 am today, Pauline had sorted the list into the collecting areas and was impatient to call at the first police station on her own route: Walworth Road, just south of the Elephant and Castle.

Pauline knows how many dogs are to be collected, but does not know what type. Neither does she know what condition they are in: they may be sick or badly injured. Her job is simply to drive the dogs to Battersea for them to be inoculated and medically checked by a waiting veterinary nurse before going into Tealby Kennels where they are required by law to be kept for seven days before being put up for sale. If a dog is sick or injured, it is taken to the Home's resident veterinary surgeon, Shaun Opperman, who treats it immediately. As soon as it is well, the dog joins the other strays in Tealby.

During those seven days, every dog is assessed for behaviour traits, so that a prospective buyer has as much information about it as possible. In some cases, the assessments show that a dog is too badly behaved or aggressive to be re-homed straight away. These dogs go to Battersea's innovative Rehabilitation Unit for three weeks' intensive treatment, designed to make them suitable for sale. Every dog has to spend seven days in Tealby – except those brought in by their owners. These are called 'gifts' and they go into the sales kennels in another building immediately.

Pauline's list tells her there is just one dog waiting at Walworth: it could be a playful mongrel pup, a timid Yorkie

An ambulance driver's pet, waits for the morning collection to begin.

11

or a ferocious Rottweiler. Either way, Pauline does not care: she has never had any fear of animals and in 21 years working for Battersea, she has learned to read dogs well and has had only the odd nip. This has as much to do with her gentle, yet assertive, approach as the dogs' own nervous uncertainty. With large, aggressive dogs, Pauline has the option to use a long pole with a rope noose to capture them from a safe distance, but resorts to this only if she has no choice.

'The minute they see the pole, they grab it and shake it about,' she says, neatly navigating the hurly-burly free-for-all of the Elephant and Castle. 'The dog is wound up and you are wound up. To me, you need to wind the dog down, get it on your side. The more you talk to them, the more you can touch and stroke them. The last thing I want is to let the dogs see I'm scared. They do know when you are afraid of them. If a dog is a quivering wreck, and shouting and screaming, and you approach it a quivering wreck yourself, the chances are that you'll get nowhere. If it's nasty and aggressive and wants to attack out of fear, the last thing you want to do is antagonize it further.

'I try to put myself in the dog's position. If I were locked up in a foreign jail and had no idea what anyone was saying to me, I wouldn't want some aggressive person coming at me with a big stick. But if someone came in with the right body language, the right attitude, and talked to me in the right tone – even if it was double Dutch – then I'd know they were being kind, and I'd be more likely to respond.'

Pauline coaxing a reluctant stray into her animal ambulance.

It is hard to imagine any animal – or human being, come to that – not responding to Pauline: she has a cheery outlook, a warm smile for everyone she meets and an infectious giggle when she sees the funny side of things. Pauline's love of life is matched by her love of dogs, which is why she gets on so well with Katie Boyle, the television personality who has served on Battersea's Committee for 25 years.

The two became friends nearly 12 years ago after Pauline wrote to the Committee, asking them to do something about the dreadful state of a number of police station kennels on her drivers' rounds. They were never cleaned out and were 'disgustingly filthy' she told them. There were no beds and dogs were not always fed. If it was cold, no one bothered

12

to provide a blanket. If it was hot, they were often not given water. Worse, many of the kennels had wooden slats on the floor and a dog could easily hang itself if its lead got caught in a slat. She had tried to improve conditions, but had got nowhere.

On behalf of the Committee, Katie tackled the problem head on. First, she joined Pauline on her rounds to see the kennels for herself. Then she used her influential contacts to ensure that action was taken to improve things.

Pauline cannot speak highly enough of Battersea's most flamboyant Committee member. 'I have never met anyone of her standing who cares so much about animals,' she says. 'She is 100 per cent committed, there's no question about that.

'When we first went out, I didn't think for a moment she would want to go into a kennel with me, particularly if the dog was difficult. But she is absolutely fearless and went straight in.

'Katie has been out hundreds of times, not only with me. At one point, it was every week. She would arrive bright and early, in a tracksuit, with stewing steak cut up into little pieces for the dogs.

'After a while, she would be out of the ambulance and into the kennel before me! Even if she was confronted by a nasty dog, jumping about and snarling, she would simply give it a handful of meat, then sit down and talk to it. She threw herself into the job, taking dogs to the ambulance on their leads, or, if they were small and frightened, carrying them. She didn't care, just did what was right for the animals. Over the past 12 years, she must have brought in hundreds of dogs. Her enthusiasm is amazing. She tells me she's 72, but I find it hard to believe. She has the energy of someone 35. She certainly wears *me* out.'

At Walworth Road, Pauline finds a black bitch Dachshund-Staffordshire Bull Terrier cross, shivering in a tiny kennel in the car park. The dog seems pleased to see her: it responds to her soft, friendly voice and gentle touch and allows Pauline to slip a lead over her head and carry her out into the rain and on to the van. Pauline ties the lead to a rail, reassures her that everything is going to be all right, then closes the rear door. Through sad eyes, the little dog looks forlornly at her, still shivering with fear at what might lie ahead.

'We pick up a lot of Staffie-types,' Pauline says. 'People get them because they look tough and are good for protection. If you are used to them, they are lovely, but if you don't know how to control them, they are quite a handful.'

If Pauline is disappointed that the dog turned out to be so docile, she does not show it; but the truth is that she prefers dealing with dogs that are harder to handle. Heading south to the next police station, Lewisham, she admits:

A WELL-MANNERED DOG

A well-behaved dog knows, and responds to, the basic commands ie. 'sit', 'down' and 'stay'.

It does not pull on the lead.

It comes back when called.

It will be happy to see you without jumping up at you.

It is amiable with children.

It is friendly to other animals.

It is house-trained and not destructive to household furniture.

'Doing the collecting is like being in the front line and I love it because I never know what the day is going to bring. But to have nice little dogs all the time would be boring. I love all dogs, but get more satisfaction removing a difficult one from an unpleasant situation and seeing it calmed down and unfrightened by the time we arrive at Battersea.'

Not that handling a difficult dog leaves Pauline calm herself. For all her confidence and courage, there have been days when the shock of what she has gone through has hit her afterwards. She has lost count of the times she has climbed into her ambulance and sat there, shaking, unable to keep her hands steady on the wheel, much less drive. These terrifying moments were in the days when it was legal to own a Pit Bull Terrier, before the restrictions imposed nowadays.

'Sometimes I'd have to get as many as four in the van in one trip,' she remembers. 'I was never scared while I was dealing with them, no matter how much they snarled and struggled and bared their teeth. But when it was all over and they were safely in the van, it would hit me just what physical danger I'd been in, and

LEFT: Two strays on their way to a warm welcome.

BELOW: Veterinary nurse, Lisa Winstanly, comforts one of Pauline's passengers as it starts a new life.

THE RIGHT DOG FOR YOU

Do not rush into things. Do your research and think about it carefully because your dog will be with you for a very long time.

Can you afford a dog and the cost of the vet's bills?

Think about your lifestyle, about how much your dog will be 'home alone', and what plans you will make when you go off on a holiday abroad?

Do you have the time to groom, train and socialize with your dog? Do you have time to give it the exercise it needs?

Is a mongrel best for you or do you want a breed? If it's a particular breed, read up on its character traits with regard to suitability with children, other animals, exercise requirements and general maintenance.

There are many wonderful dogs at Battersea to choose from, and great care is taken 'matchmaking' you with the right dog.

I'd begin to shake. There's nothing quite like an angry Pit Bull to give you the shakes!'

Walworth and Lewisham are the first of five calls Pauline has to make this Monday. There are just five dogs to be collected – a huge difference from the Mondays Pauline experienced when she joined Battersea in 1977. With no Sunday collection, as there is now, the average number of dogs collected was between 80 and 100, levelling out to 40 or so for the rest of the week.

'The high number of dogs made it far more emotionally draining for us,' says Pauline. 'If we didn't have enough room for all the dogs, we had to go back for the ones we'd left. By the end of the day, we were shattered.'

In those days, Battersea took in around 20,000 dogs every year. Now, with the introduction of council-employed dog wardens, who often re-home dogs themselves, the number has dropped to around 10,000. An average of twelve dogs a day are picked up by the four animal ambulances.

Understandably, the sorry spectacles Pauline has witnessed over 21 years have made her cynical about humans. Many dogs she has picked up have been emaciated through months of neglect; some have been horribly scarred by hot oil or fat thrown over them. One little mongrel even had one of its front paws squashed flat from the ankle. It was a sight that haunted Pauline for weeks.

'You would have thought someone could have seen the pain the poor creature was in and taken it to a vet, but they just dumped it at Camberwell police station,' she sighs, with a despairing shake of the head. 'I took the dog to our vet, who felt there was nothing he could do but amputate. I was terribly sad, but, in the long run, I'm sure it was for the best. A totally flat paw was useless and probably agony.'

There are dozens of upsetting stories, but another that lingers in her memory is the call she received from Catford police station one Christmas Day, after she had been on the road for five hours, collecting more than 60 dogs. Waiting at the station were ten black mongrel puppies. They had been dumped there in a cardboard box.

Thankfully, Pauline's cynicism has not hardened her. If anything, she says, all the hurt and pain she has witnessed have made her softer. 'If I was as hard as nails and didn't give a damn, I'd be in the wrong job,' she says. 'You can't work with dogs and not be compassionate. After 21 years, I'm soppier than ever with them. And I'm glad it's that way.'

Seeking a short cut to Lewisham, to avoid the ever-increasing snarl of the morning rush hour, Pauline's hands-free phone rings: she often gets calls en route, telling her to divert to one police station or another to deal with emergency cases. To her relief, this is only a query and she continues on her journey.

At Lewisham, a young crossbred German Shepherd – no more than 18 months old – is whimpering; too scared, it seems, to want to leave its kennel. Again Pauline's soft, reassuring voice does the trick: within minutes the dog is on a lead, following her through the rain to the van. He jumps in willingly, glad to see another dog there. After a night alone, it seems he is pleased to have some company.

What a difference from the last time Pauline was at Lewisham. Then, a huge Rottweiler was so wound up it was throwing itself at the bars of its kennel, intent, it appeared, on biting anyone who came near. Displaying an indifference she did not feel, Pauline opened the kennel door. She slipped a lead over the dog's head. Miraculously, it calmed down immediately.

'I was careful not to look at him, though,' Pauline says. 'I just walked out and led him to the van. I made sure I had no physical contact with him out in the open. I would have had no protection. Once he was in the van and tied securely to the rail, I felt safer and able to stroke him. The more I did, the better the dog felt and, by the time we got to Battersea, he was quite docile.'

For the Home's longest-serving driver, helping dogs is a pleasure no money in the world can buy. Pauline likes money as much as anyone, but insists it is not her motivation. She puts it simply, but sincerely: 'As long as I can go out every day, knowing I can hug a dog, money isn't important. If I won a few million on the Lottery and was told that a condition of banking the money was that I must never touch another dog, I wouldn't want a penny.'

At South Norwood, Pauline collects one of those Greyhound crossbreeds, known as Lurchers, then drives to Banstead, in Surrey, for a Terrier-Spaniel cross. Finally she heads for Mitcham, where the most adorable black mongrel puppy – no more than six months old – is waiting, its deep brown, trusting eyes showing all the curiosity and interest of youth, not the hurt and disillusionment of betrayal Pauline has seen so often. She gives him a cuddle, then places him in one of the four cages on the left side of the van for his protection. As she closes the door, the puppy is looking in wide-eyed wonder at the German Shepherd straining at his lead to mount the Lurcher.

Approaching Battersea, Pauline notices she is low on petrol and pulls into a petrol station near the Home, where she normally fills up. Once she has unloaded the morning's collections, she may have to go out again on an emergency, and she needs to know she has a full tank. Out of habit, she takes the keys out of the ignition and puts them in a pocket. It is something she has never failed to do since a Saturday morning three years before, when a man, in his mid-twenties and high on drugs, jumped into the van while she was filling up and drove off with eight dogs in the back.

'I couldn't believe it,' Pauline says. 'I was only a few feet away, with the nozzle in the tank. A little man, smaller even than me, was about to get into his two-seater sports car and I screeched at him: "Follow that van!"

'I sounded like a hysterical witch, but he didn't question me – he had seen what happened. He told me to jump in.

'"The guy can't get far," I said. "I'd only put a pound's worth of petrol in."

'We tore along the Embankment, towards Vauxhall, like a scene from *Starsky and Hutch*, overtaking one car after another, until we were only a couple of cars behind the van. I'd never been so frightened. As it went round Lambeth roundabout, the van was going so fast it toppled over and crashed. To my horror, I saw a Jack Russell leap out of a huge hole in the side and dash off. My first instinct was to run after him, but I was also worried for the other dogs, some of whom were tied up, and might be in distress.

'Frantic with worry, I jumped out. I sprinted towards the van, screaming loudly. Some big bloke grabbed me in a bear-hug, probably thinking I was a nosey passer-by wanting to get involved in something nothing to do with me. I shouted at him to let go, then booted him in the leg to make sure he did.

'I ran to the van and opened the rear door. I was relieved all the dogs were unharmed. The only hurt was in their eyes. As far as they were concerned, I was the driver responsible. And they all looked at me, as if to say: "Was that *really* necessary?"

'As I was checking the dogs, some people were round the front of the van, getting the driver out. He ran off before I could get my hands on him. Just as well. After what he had put my dogs through, I felt like killing him.'

Fortunately, in his rush to escape, the thief left a bag in the van, containing his personal details, and he was later arrested. Unfortunately, the Jack Russell was never apprehended.

It is coming up to ten o'clock as Pauline turns off Chelsea Bridge and drives through the electronically controlled gates at the back of the Dogs' Home. Crossing wasteland newly acquired by the Home for redevelopment, she passes a line of kennels for dogs on medication, and parks at the rear of Tealby Kennels. One by one, she takes her five strays into the receiving bay, where a veterinary nurse, Lisa Winstanly, gives them an inoculation and a check-over.

It is still bitterly cold and windy. It is still raining. But for the five strays, the welcome is warm and friendly and, as they are led up to kennels in the clean, bright building bearing Mary Tealby's name, Pauline goes into her office at the rear of the building and writes out everything the police have reported about each dog – its description, where and when it was found, whether it is pregnant or has been in an accident etc. – for Battersea's computerized Dog Register, and for the hand-written card that is put up on the front of each dog's kennel. It is crucial information that signals the start of their lives as Battersea dogs.

From now on, they will be well fed, kept warm and comforted by devoted, conscientious staff. If they become ill – as is likely, with kennel cough –they will be treated with kindness and the latest medical equipment, in conditions that would be the envy of many vets throughout the country.

CHAPTER TWO

A dog's life! Only the best will do

Ever since it moved from north London to Battersea in 1871, the Dogs' Home has always had a mystique. Even locals grew up wondering: what *does* go on behind those big doors? Many did not know the Home was open to the public; those who did were unaware dogs *and cats* were sold there. Certainly few knew that the Home was controlled by a committee of well-connected animal lovers, eager to ensure that the work started by Mary Tealby continued in the way they felt she would have wanted.

With the welfare of the animals always first in their minds, the Committee have always done their best to keep up with the times, but money was always a problem. As a charity, Battersea relies on legacies and donations from the public and at times there were rarely enough of either for the Committee to do everything they knew the Home needed.

With as many as 900 dogs there at any one time, contagious diseases, such as kennel cough, were always a serious threat. Probably what was needed, even more than replacing the hundreds of old kennels, was a full-time veterinary surgeon. By the early eighties, Battersea's financial picture was brighter so the Committee were able to appoint one – William Wadman-Taylor, who, with his wife, Ruth, was given the job of managing the Home under its Secretary, Colonel Henry Sweeney. Over the next six years, there was such a substantial increase in income that the Committee were also able to give the go ahead for one of the most exciting developments in Battersea's history: a modern four-storey building with 117 kennels. It would cost £3 million, but new kennels were long overdue and everyone at the home felt the building was well worth the money.

Fittingly, it was decided to call the building Tealby Kennels as a tribute to Battersea's much respected founder.

The Home continued to change and progress with the times. New developments were constantly being considered because there was always room for modernization and improvement. In 1992, a year after the Queen opened Tealby, the Committee had to appoint a new Director General for the home to replace Colonel Sweeney who was due to retire. If they were to build on his achievements, continue the progress throughout the 1990s and into the next millennium, they needed someone dynamic, with experience in business – as well as a genuine commitment to the care of dogs and cats.

The man they wanted, a retired Lieutenant Colonel, Duncan Green, was a youthful forty-seven and open for any interesting challenges. When he was first approached, he was not interested; he wanted to work for himself, not a charity. But after talking it over with his wife, Juliette, he decided to go to Battersea to have a look around and find out precisely what the job entailed.

The Committee chairman, Tom Field-Fisher Q.C. was so impressed with Duncan that a few weeks later, in September, he asked him to go back for an official interview in front of five members. They liked him so much he was asked back a third time to meet the full Committee and they all agreed he was the man they were were looking for.

What the Committee did not know was that Duncan wanted to run Battersea as much as they wanted him to. After the September interview, he had gone back for a look around and had become absorbed with the place. The Home was just the challenge he was looking for and he took over on 15 January 1993.

After he was appointed, one of the first decisions the Committee sanctioned was to make the public reception area in Tealby Kennels a more welcoming place for people who had come to part with their pets. Within a couple of months a new indoor reception area was introduced.

At the same time, Battersea's re-homing procedure was reviewed. The questionnaire that prospective buyers had to complete before being interviewed – which consisted of twelve basic questions – was updated to ensure it had more relevant facts that would prevent people from leaving with dogs unsuited to their lifestyles.

There was also a need to re-examine the way in which puppies were cared for. The few that arrived at Battersea needed to be brought up in as near a domestic situation as possible, ideally with other puppies, rather like a litter. So a puppy house was intro-duced – a warm, cosy room where the young arrivals were encouraged to put their traumas behind them and run around and play like puppies are supposed to. The room resembled a children's nursery, with bright mobiles hanging from the ceiling, huge, colourful pictures decorating the walls and toys – including a slide! – all over the place.

THE TRUTH ABOUT THE DOGS' HOME BATTERSEA

It is a myth that dogs are put down after seven days. Dogs are kept for as long as it takes to find a home for them.

Some dogs are put down when they are very old, ill or incurably aggressive. No healthy dog is put down.

The Home was founded in 1860 at Holloway, not Battersea, as 'The Temporary Home for Lost and Starving Dogs'.

The Dogs' Home has taken in cats since 1883, but initially half the cats were private boarders.

Queen Victoria became patron in 1885. The present patron is Her Majesty Queen Elizabeth II.

The largest number of dogs ever admitted in one year was 35,064, in 1886.

Battersea has supplied dogs to royalty, the police, HM Customs, hearing dogs for the deaf and many other organizations.

ABOVE: The best job in the world? Looking after a roomful of puppies in the purpose-built nursery.

OPPOSITE: A new arrival puts his personality on parade.

In play, the puppies were taught to understand body language and social skills: those that had been so frightened and confused when they arrived that they attacked other pups, were sharing the same food bowl with them a few days later. They were paper-trained to go to the toilet, taught basic commands – such as 'sit' and 'stay' – and introduced to everyday noises, not only washing machines, vacuum cleaners and music, but also the deafening din of trains, which thundered above the puppy house throughout the day. The youngsters got used to being fussed over by people, too: their house was away from the reception area, out of sight of visitors, but most of Battersea's staff soon found the opportunity of a lunchtime cuddle too hard to resist.

Soon after Duncan Green's arrival, it was decided to invest £6 million in another new building – primarily for dogs and cats ready for re-homing – and to

use Tealby Kennels only as a seven-day holding block for strays. The new building, which would replace the old ground-level kennels on the east side, would be named Kent Kennels after the Home's President, Prince Michael of Kent.

Six firms of architects were taken on a tour of the Home so that each knew what the requirements were for the new kennels. Their unique brief was to design bright, airy and well-equipped, customer-friendly kennels where the dogs would be as happy as possible.

The innovative new kennels were also to have state-of-the-art toilets. Duncan Green personally designed a loo which enabled staff to sweep dog mess into a sewage pipe, hidden below a stainless steel cover in every one of the 164 kennels, then flush it away like a domestic toilet.

Heating in the kennels was a top priority too: if two dogs shared a kennel, with a small heat source, the more dominant one would go to where it was warmest and deprive the other of heat. Long heaters were installed inside the wall in the bed area so that the dogs could adjust their own position and get the amount of heat they wanted.

With customers in mind, the kennels had to have clean, light corridors that did not recycle the same air. They needed to be staff friendly, too, because the more time *they* spent on mundane cleaning chores, the less they had for the vitally-important socializing with the dogs.

However good the new kennels might look to the public it was considered very important that the dogs looked their best too. The more appealing a dog looked the better chance it had of attracting an owner. To begin with a professional groomer was employed for one day a week but soon it became clear that the Home needed a full-time groomer. At the same time, one of the kennel hands, Claire Barnes, showed great interest in grooming. One morning, she was summoned to Duncan's office. 'Come on, then,' he said, smiling. 'What do you need?' He put her in touch with a grooming company and told her to choose the equipment she needed for a grooming room on every floor of Kent Kennels. Claire could not have been more thrilled with her boss's response. She joyfully bought super-jet stand dryers, hydraulic tables, collapsible cages, drying cabinets, brushes, combs, clippers and various shampoos and conditioners.

In making the new kennels as modern as possible, every tiny detail was taken into consideration. Even the metal used for the kennel bars was stainless steel at substantial extra cost.

The appointed architects reported once a fortnight so every detail could be checked – from the size of the reception and shape of the desks, to the planned flow of visitors. The building sub-committee met fortnightly as well to approve the drawings. Plans progressed smoothly.

Kent Kennels, the six million pound building that prepared Battersea for the next millennium. On the left, the former cattery, Whittington Lodge.

One of the biggest worries that then faced the Committee and staff before the builders moved in was to find alternative accommodation for the dogs and cats – particularly the sick ones having treatment. By luck, plans to widen the M25 on the Berkshire-Surrey border were being delayed and a kennelling business – Cambridge Kennels – became available at Egham in Surrey, near Bell Mead, the country house in seven acres of grassland, which Battersea bought as an 'overflow' annexe 20 years ago. Cambridge Kennels had to be brought up to Battersea's standards, but there was room for 180 dogs and the Committee quickly gave the arrangement the green light. Fifty dogs were earmarked for Bell Mead, temporary kennels were built on new land at the rear of Battersea to house the rest, and, early that year, 1995, the bulldozers moved in to pull the old kennels down. For the next 18 months, the Home was a mess: lorries, plant machinery and workmen were all over the place; the noise was deafening; dust got in everywhere; and, of course, there were still some dogs kennelled there.

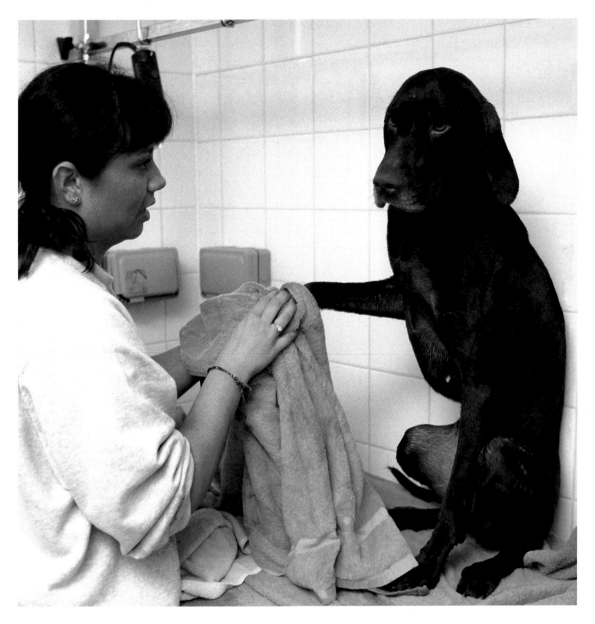

LEFT AND ABOVE: He may not like it, but after Claire's professional make-over he is ready for his public appearance.

The staff had to work round the building site. They did not mind one bit and coped admirably. They knew the inconvenience was going to be worth it. For them – and the animals in their care.

Meanwhile the Committee appointed a new manager for the Home, Nichola Vickers. She had been in the Army for seven years, rising to the rank of captain. She was 31 years old, bright and articulate with managerial skills. And, having a military background, she talked the same language as her boss.

Within a few months, Nichola could see that Battersea's operation, while adequate, needed some streamlining to realize its full potential. Her experience in managing people helped, but because she was new she was also able to look at the workings of the Home objectively from an outsider's viewpoint.

To try to improve relations between management and staff, Nichola took over the board room to interview workers individually. She was keen to convince them that they should not be frightened of her; that she wanted to make their jobs easier and the lives of the animals better.

One afternoon, a member of staff Nichola had noticed wandering about the Home suddenly appeared, unannounced in the middle of a meeting. He did not seem wary or distrustful of her in any way; nor frightened. He made no sound, just walked slowly around her, wondering what she was doing. Then he left, as silently as he arrived, seemingly satisfied. Racoon, the large, overweight Labrador who was the Home's yard dog – a mascot given the run of the place – saw nothing to worry about at all. He behaved as though Nichola was a positive addition.

On the day the dogs moved into Kent Kennels in October 1996, Duncan was returning from a four-day International Animal Welfare conference in Budapest. Driving out of Heathrow, he switched on the radio and, by coincidence, Battersea's public relations consultant, Stephen Danos, was being interviewed about the new kennels. A tingle of pleasure ran through Duncan: so the dogs were in.

Normally, after an overseas trip, Duncan would not have gone to Battersea until the next day, but Stephen's interview thrilled him and he could not wait to see the kennels. He dropped off his suitcase at home and headed towards Battersea. He was excited, but nervous, too: so much care had been taken to get the building right, he was certain the staff and the public would love it. But what about the dogs? They were the important ones. What would they think?

That afternoon, most of the dogs were out on a charity walk for cancer in Battersea Park and the Home was strangely quiet. Duncan walked into the bright, new building, trying hard not to let anyone see how nervous he was, and went up the ramp to the first floor. The first dog he saw was a Lurcher, a beautiful, big, white one, tall and regal, and she was sitting on the ledge above her bed, happy and content, looking around her, almost proudly.

Duncan felt a lump in his throat and swallowed hard. The look of that lovely Lurcher told him all he wanted to know. Everything was going to be fine. All the slog was going to be worth it, not only for that Lurcher, but for all the other unwanted dogs picked up off the streets and brought to Battersea by Pauline Martignetti and her colleagues.

CHAPTER THREE

What *really* happens in the first seven days

Even today, many people believe that lost and abandoned dogs are taken to Battersea and put to sleep. But that is a myth. Tealby Kennels, where all strays spend their first seven days, is *not* Death Row: it is merely a temporary home before they are put in the shop window of Kent Kennels for re-homing.

The reason the myth was created is probably because of the seven-day period Battersea is required by law to keep the strays, to give their owners a chance to claim them. People assumed that if a dog was unclaimed during that time, there was no alternative but to end its life. The truth is that Battersea's main purpose is to re-home *every* dog taken there. And every re-homable dog *is* found a home. The only dogs put to sleep are those on their last legs and in distress, ones which are not re-homable because they have too much wrong with them, or those which are too aggressive to be re-homed.

Veterinary surgeon Shaun Opperman restoring a newly-arrived stray 'to its former glory.'

Dogs which arrive fit and well go to kennels on Tealby immediately. Those ill, or badly injured, are taken to the Home's veterinary surgeon, Shaun Opperman, a gentle, softly-spoken man in his early thirties, who gives them the quickest, most caring, expert treatment to make them well enough for re-homing.

For Shaun, the job is highly rewarding, particularly when his skill on the operating table saves a dog everyone has given up for dead, and he later sees a photograph of it running around in a new home. On the other hand, it can be sad and upsetting when a dog is brought in, suffering, and Shaun is forced to wait seven days before giving it the peaceful and dignified end he feels it deserves.

'I get upset, but I get angry, too,' he said. 'The owners have been given years of endless pleasure by their dogs and should be making the decision themselves to end their lives. But you get the impression they don't want to pay the last vet bill. They know if they abandon their dog and it is brought here, it will be done for free.'

What also angers Shaun are those owners who bring in perfectly healthy – and re-homable – dogs to be put to sleep because they are going abroad.

'A lot of people are selfish enough to think their dogs can't live without them,' Shaun said. 'We refuse to do what they ask. We are not an out-patients for euthanasia. If we were, we'd be putting every old dog to sleep within ten miles of here. What we ask people to do is sign over their dog to the Home, for us to do what we think is right. If it is re-homable, every effort is made to find a new owner. If it is not, then we do put it to sleep. I may be tempted to get annoyed with people who bring in old dogs, but I can't. At least they are bringing them in, not dumping them in a park or on a motorway!'

Shaun has been at Battersea since 1992 and has had to put many animals to sleep. He has not become callous or immune to it and says he never will. But he has developed a professional detachment that enables him not to become sentimentally involved with cases.

'I have a love of animals, naturally, but I have a deep respect, too,' he said. 'When I'm putting an old or diseased dog – who is not re-homable – to sleep, I know I'm doing the right thing – and why I'm doing it.'

Kennel cough, caused by a variety of bugs, is a problem in all kennels, and Battersea has its fair share. To a healthy dog in a loving home it will usually be a soft cough, but to stressed, nervous and undernourished dogs, living in overcrowded conditions, it can infect the chest and lead to complications.

Most dogs are exposed to kennel cough during their seven days in Tealby. Usually, they have a bit of a temperature and a runny nose and get better themselves after a couple of weeks. But when complications develop, Shaun is called in. When he started at Battersea he had to put 400 dogs to sleep every year because of kennel cough, but now, even those with bronchial pneumonia are treated in intensive care and recover.

'Half our energies are spent coping with kennel cough complications and because treatment is now available, no dog with kennel cough is ever put to sleep,' Shaun said. 'Unfortunately, the disease is always present within the

MEDICAL EMERGENCIES

Always register with a local vet. Remember to do it when you move house.

Read up on essential first aid for your dog. Lots of books are available.

Make up your own first aid box for your dog.

Phone your vet ahead to allow preparation for your arrival.

Stay calm.

For suspected poisoning, keep the packaging to show the vet. Seek advice before attempting to induce vomiting.

Home and very hard to vaccinate against. To clear it from the Home, we would have to move all the dogs out.'

Rarely will a dog show no signs of kennel cough, but, earlier this year, a three-month-old mongrel puppy that had been re-homed was brought back by its new owner, suffering from bronchial pneumonia, brought on by the disease. The puppy was put on intravenous fluids and antibiotics, given extra oxygen, and hand-fed by a nurse, who took him home with her every night. It was touch and go for four days, but, happily, the puppy pulled through. The owner was shown how to feed the dog with a syringe and it made a full recovery.

It is difficult to make dogs with kennel cough eat, so Shaun has introduced a microwave in the medical unit's kitchen, in which nurses heat up sausages, chicken, fish and any leftovers they can scrounge from the canteen. Some dogs feel so miserable and depressed, however, that they cannot be bothered to eat. To encourage them, nursing staff often hold a piece of sausage above the dog's head, then drop it on the floor in front of the dog, pretending it is a game. Invariably, it works.

Such is the total involvement of the nurses in their jobs that many break down in floods of tears at some of the harrowing sights they have to deal with. Earlier this year, one little mongrel, brought in by the police, was crawling with maggots. Another, little more than a skeleton, lived for only five days because he was so undernourished his kidneys were rotten. Unbelievably, some dogs arrive with their ears chopped off.

For Shaun, a big attraction of being Battersea's vet is that he is not dealing with an owner or his or her financial position; the Home is well-enough funded so that he is always able to get on and do what he feels is right for a dog. This has one drawback, however; all vets are taught in training to ask the owners for their animal's history but, in most cases, Shaun will not know what has happened to the dog he is treating. 'I only have the symptoms in front of me, and have to rely on past experience and back-up laboratory facilities, such as blood tests, radiographs etc.,' he said.

Shaun is also able to perform minor cosmetic surgery to enhance a dog's chances of being re-homed. He might, for example, remove a wart, or a growth – even give the dog's teeth a scale and polish to make its breath sweeter.

'I'm always looking at ways to do nips and tucks to restore dogs to their former glory before they go up for sale,' he said. 'I'm sure it makes them feel better.'

The downside of his job is that Shaun has the unenviable task of deciding the fate of the animal – and of comforting heartbroken staff who may not agree with him. Groomer Claire Barnes remembers battling with him over a lovely German Shepherd, about seven years old, who had come into Battersea in the worst state she had ever seen any dog in her eight years at the Home.

Claire, like Shaun, does all she can to transform ill-treated dogs to the way

they once looked. Often, they will arrive with their overgrown coats a foot wide and matted fur covering their eyes. She clips them immediately, gives them a bath and, more often than not, they end up running around like two-year-olds. She felt the same about the Shepherd. It would take all her patience to restore *him* to his former glory, but he was such a handsome dog, she was determined to do it.

ABOVE: One of Shaun's patients being drip fed intravenously.

OVERLEAF: Two dogs compare their wounds after surgery.

Claire did not know for sure where the German Shepherd had lived all his life, but suspected it was outside in a motor mechanics' yard, because the poor creature was covered from head to toe in oil, which had seeped through to his stomach, making the skin red. He had lain in wet cement which had dried, leaving his tail and the fur inside his legs, stiff.

Normally, Claire takes half an hour to groom a dog, but she set aside a day for this one. Before bathing him, she had to smother the dog with the green jelly used by mechanics to remove grease from their hands. She massaged him for hours to clean his fur. She had to cut off the dried cement. It took her six hours before the dog was ready for the bath.

WHAT TO DO IF YOU
LOSE YOUR DOG

It is a traumatic experience,
but stay calm.

Have faith – most pet owners
are reunited with their dogs.

Phone your local police
station, vet and local dog
warden (ring 192 if you don't
have the numbers).

If you live in London, phone
the Dogs' Home Battersea on
0171 622 3626.

The National Strays Bureau
collate details of all dogs lost
and found around the
country. They have a high
success rate.

Spread the word.
Ask neighbours, local shop
keepers etc.
Put local notices up.

Don't give up. Keep looking.

'He kept getting fed up and I'd take him for little walks,' said Claire. 'By five-thirty, when he was all dry, his black and tan coat came up gorgeously. He was transformed. The only sad sight was his tail, which was totally bald, because I'd had to shave it to get off all the cement. His skin was still a bit red, but he looked lovely and I was confident we could find him a home, probably with the woman who had found him. She was married to a vet and she had written on a card that, if he was not claimed, she and her husband would have him.

'Unfortunately, I was wrong. Without all his fur, I could see that the dog's hips were bad and his back was thin, as though there had been some muscle wastage. Also, both ears were badly inflamed and he could barely hear.

'Shaun said the dog needed major operations on his ears, and we had to consider whether it was fair to put him through it, at his age, particularly as he would then have the stress of settling in to a new home. Then there was the obvious problem with his hips. And, of course, we could not be sure just how much of the oil had poisoned his system.

'We decided to delay making a decision and for the next five days I made sure the dog was as comfortable as possible. I took him for little walks and he looked fine. But I could see he was never going to be a really fit dog.

'It had to be Shaun's decision and finally he said it was kinder to put the dog to sleep. I didn't agree and battled hard to save him, but, deep down, I knew he was right. It broke my heart – and the woman who wanted to have him was devastated. I was dreadfully upset, but consoled myself that the dog had had five days of comfort, all clean and smelling lovely, with someone he knew loved him.'

Happily, Shaun's success rate vastly outweighs the sad failures. In his time at Battersea, he has lost count of the number of dogs, seemingly on the way out, who have lived to bark another day. One that springs to mind is Pauline Martignetti's mongrel, Billy, which she brought in barely able to breathe, after being beaten and kicked by three youths.

Amazingly, Billy had no broken bones or internal bleeding, but he was black and blue and his windpipe was smashed: he kept retching and vomiting and was unable to eat. Shaun took X-rays and discovered Billy's trachea – a tube, held open by rings of cartilage – was like a mangled drinking straw: the rings were crushed and splintered, making it difficult for him to suck or swallow. To save the dog, Shaun had to perform a stabilizing operation he had never done before: he had to cut a plastic cylinder into tiny rings, then open the dog's neck and stitch them around the trachea to support it.

For Shaun, it was a delicate, scary operation because of the vital and sensitive tissues around the trachea, but Billy came through it well. Pauline insisted on looking after him until he was fully recovered and became so attached, she decided to keep him. Six months later, however, the dog had difficulty breathing again and Pauline took him back to Shaun, fearfully worried that, this time, there would be nothing he could do. Shaun had to take out all the plastic rings, but, happily, the trachea had healed and he was able to solve what breathing problems the dog had. Billy is now back on the road with Pauline, happy and content – and breathing easily.

Shaun remembers Billy affectionately: 'He's a lovely dog and the nurses and I felt good after we sorted him out,' he says. 'We get an endless list of average cases – such as neutering – and, because they are like a conveyor belt, we get used to them. But then we get an operation like Billy's, which involves lots of staff, and everyone's morale is high.'

Lucky, the 12-year-old crossbred Labrador brought in with her son, who had a sinister-looking lump on his hind leg, was another such dog. Shaun and his team were so concerned about removing the lump that they did not notice a swelling in his mum's tummy until the dogs were re-homed and the new owner brought her back. Shaun found the swelling was caused by a tumour on the spleen, stretching from the chest to the far end of the abdomen, which had pushed all the other organs to the side. Happily, it was not malignant. But it still needed a long, painstaking operation to remove the enormous aubergine mass.

'It was another fiddly operation,' Shaun said. 'Tumours like that have many vessels and it took two hours cutting off each one and easing the mass out of the wound. We had to be careful not to puncture it and cause a haemorrhage, because that could have been fatal. As it was, everything went well and, after a couple of days on a drip, Lucky went home, with a spring in her step for being quite a bit slimmer!'

Dogs do not show signs of having such a tumour until it gets so big that they have trouble breathing. Lucky's owner noticed hers only when the dog rolled on to her back.

Shaun was confident of saving Billy and Lucky, but there have been times when he felt that, no matter what he did, the animal brought to him was going to die. He did not give Roland a chance. The ageing German Shepherd was attacked one morning by three other dogs while on exercise, and badly bitten around the neck and chest and under a foreleg. His colour was dreadful. He was gasping. And his temperature was 108.

OVERLEAF: Even puppies are handed in to Battersea by the public, but some are born in the Home.

**HOW NOT TO LOSE
YOUR DOG**

Have a disc attached to
the collar with an up-to-date
phone number
and/or address.
(This is required by law.)

Watch it like a hawk! Don't let
it wander on its own. Be
careful about leaving it outside
shops.

Take care when your dog is in
season. She might not go
missing, but other dogs might
get lost chasing her.

Keep photographs.
You will be glad of them if you
lose your dog.

Put your dog on the Internet.
With its own home page on
the worldwide web, you may
find it more quickly,
if it goes missing.

Best of all, use a microchip,
painlessly implanted under the
skin at the back of the neck. It
contains all the details of your
dog and is 100 per cent safe
and reliable.

'He was nearly dead,' said Shaun. 'If he'd had to be driven 20 minutes to a local vet, I don't think he would have made it. But we have wonderful facilities here and were able to act immediately. We poured surgical spirit on Roland's coat to bring his temperature down outside, and gave him a cold water enema to cool him down inside. Then we gave him oxygen to help his breathing and put him on an intravenous drip to ease the trauma.'

For the next eight hours, it was touch and go: Roland was clinging to life, but his breathing was worryingly laboured and Shaun and his team feared they might lose him at any time. Thankfully, Roland's fighting spirit pulled him through and, by evening, he was a lot brighter. He was very uncomfortable over the next few days and had to be given painkillers and antibiotics. Then he developed kennel cough and a huge abscess under the foreleg, which had to be drained off. But he is out of the woods. With every day, the memory of that savage, unprovoked attack seems to be fading. He is going to make it.

Another puppy, a cross Lurcher bitch called Rhubarb, was brought in with a hideous wound on a hind leg after being hit by a car. She was in such pain that she was snappy and nervous and would not let anyone near her for two days. Finally, Shaun had to amputate the leg. This, it seems, bothered the staff more than Rhubarb herself, because the next day she was running around as if nothing had happened. Jade Hall, a kennel hand, later took her home every night for several weeks, to teach her some manners, because she had become very dominant, and even more snappy. She soon calmed down and was re-homed to a family with a Shar Pei.

More amputations are performed at Battersea than in a general veterinary practice, because Shaun sees dogs at a very late stage, often after someone else has attempted to repair the damage. 'Our job is a salvaging operation, but it is very rewarding,' Shaun said. 'Dogs have none of our social complications. If a human woke up from surgery without a limb, it would be a physical and emotional catastrophe, but dogs just get up and bound off, as if to say, "What's the problem – I've got three other legs!" Obviously, it is better for a dog to lose a hind leg than a front one because it's the front legs that take their weight.'

Dogs handed in by loving owners, who are, for whatever reason, unable to look after them anymore, are known as 'gifts'. Battersea is not required to hold 'gift' dogs for the statutory seven days, so it is in everyone's interest to re-home them quickly, before they catch kennel cough. Such dogs are brought in for a variety of reasons, some of which can be quite moving, as May Whammond, a tough, plain-speaking Scot, discovered.

May said: 'Two chaps in their late twenties came in with a beautiful Alsatian. They were crying. One of them said he was ill and couldn't look after the dog anymore.

'I asked: "Why doesn't your partner look after it till you get better?"

'"I'm not going to get better," he said, through his tears. "I've got AIDS."

'It turned out that the two guys worked together and had been sacked because one of them had AIDS, which was a stigma at the time. The poor man's partner, who had bought the Alsatian, could not cope with a demanding dog while his friend was dying. But they loved the dog so much they wanted it to go to a good home, where it would be happy.

'It is well known here that I'm not tolerant of people and have more time for animals. But that man's honesty touched me and, after I'd taken the dog and he turned to go, I shook his hand and gave him a hug. "I do hope you don't have to suffer," I said.

'He forced a weak smile. "Why can't more people be like you?" he said.

'I wasn't very involved in re-homing "gifts" and don't remember what happened to that Alsatian. But he was such a beautiful pedigree, we would have put him up for sale almost immediately. I do hope he found a loving home. He deserved to.'

Handing over an animal you cherish to someone you have never met, entrusting its future well-being to them, is a difficult and emotionally painful experience. One woman, who had not been to Battersea before, could not bring herself to do it, and was spotted, waiting in the courtyard, outside reception, one busy afternoon, carrying a Border Collie puppy.

Ann Challis, one of Battersea's home visitors who checks out prospective buyers, was helping out with interviews. She went out to tell the woman she was not allowed to give the dog away to a new owner herself.

Ann was diplomatic, but the woman, who was in her early twenties, reacted defensively, saying she was being accused of doing something wrong. But then she broke down and started sobbing. Ann took her into an interview room and talked to her, gently, to find out what the problem was. It appeared that since buying the puppy, the young woman's nine-month-old baby son had started having bad asthma attacks. He had been taken to hospital and her husband did not want him home until the puppy was out of the house.

'The husband had told her to take the dog to Battersea and not bring it back,' Ann recalled. 'The poor girl was devastated. She didn't want to part with it but knew she had to. It was breaking her heart. She didn't have any idea how

Battersea worked, but had come here because she knew that was where she'd find people who wanted a dog. Rather than just hand the puppy over to someone behind a desk, she wanted to give it personally to someone wanting a dog. She needed to see where it was going.

'She had been outside the home for several hours, apparently, plucking up courage to come in. I don't think she knew she was doing anything wrong. She could not see anything other than that she was letting the dog down.

'She cried so much and I felt very choked. I've got children and dogs and I love them all. But you must keep things in perspective. In her case, the baby had to come first.'

Sometimes owners 'gift' dogs, not for their own sake, but for others'. A couple who brought in a gorgeous Labrador/Boxer cross, for example, desperately wanted to keep him; but, at just ten months, he had grown too big for their small house. The dog would play in the garden with the couple's two children but when they went inside, he was forced to stay outside. Understandably, he was very confused and barked incessantly – which did not go down well with the neighbours.

To keep the peace, the couple had to make a choice: upset their children by getting rid of the dog, or infuriate the neighbours further by keeping it. In this case, the couple's loss was another's gain, because the adorable creature was re-homed within a month.

That couple had made a genuine, if silly, mistake and saw Battersea as the ideal solution to their problem.

But there are other, less honourable, people who use Battersea for their own ends – cheats, who openly flout the seven-day 'no sale' law to avoid paying kennel fees. If someone with a dog wants to go away on a long weekend, they simply hand the dog in at a police station, pretending it is not theirs, then pick it up from Battersea when they get back. They will have to pay the Home £7.25 a day, plus £5 for vaccinations, but that can be cheaper than a boarding kennels.

Paul Wilkins, a 28-year-old south Londoner, now working in reception, remembers a man in his sixties who arrived time and again, drunk, to collect a golden Labrador. He would go into a pub and 'earn' his drinking money by selling the dog, knowing it would run away and end up at Battersea. The staff were tolerant for a while, but finally got fed up and warned him that if the dog came in again, they would not let him have it back. They never saw either of them again.

Battersea holds dogs and cats for people who are arrested and taken to court. But even this is open to abuse because the seven-day 'no sale' law does not apply in such cases and the animals remain the owners' property. When the owners are released and come to collect their pets, they do not have to pay the kennelling or vaccination fee: the police do, or rather, the taxpayer does albeit at a reduced rate of £5.99 a day!

Naturally, the police do not like animals being locked up longer than necessary. If an owner is likely to be jailed for, say, more than two or three months, they are sent a letter, giving them 28 days to make other arrangements for their pet. If they cannot, or will not, the animal is officially handed over to Battersea and immediately put up for sale. Often, owners who do not want their pets anymore take the easy way out: they simply wait for the police letter to arrive, then throw it in the bin, knowing that, 28 days later, the animal will become someone else's responsibility.

The Labrador/Boxer cross, 'gifted' to Battersea because his barking upset the neighbours.

Such people infuriate Kirsty Walker, Deputy Head of Kennels, who, in eight years at Battersea, has heard all the excuses, seen all the dodges. But not all those she has encountered have been hard-hearted and selfish, or deliberately out to cheat the system.

'I learned long ago not to judge a book by its cover,' she said. 'Some of the hard nuts who come in here are soft and highly responsible where their pets are concerned. A few months ago, a Weimaraner and her puppy were brought in as prisoners' property. When we examined them we discovered the puppy was ill and needed special medication. The dogs were here for two weeks while

43

Kirsty Walker, Deputy Head of Kennels, was reduced to tears by an old man's devotion to his dogs.

the owner was banged up. As soon as he was released, he was on the phone, desperately worried about "his babies". When he arrived, in jogging bottoms and sweatshirt, covered in tattoos, and looking a real geezer, I half expected him to say we could keep the puppy, as it was going to cost him a fortune in vet's bills. But he was carrying all the right tablets and could not wait to be with the dogs he obviously adored. Like a lot of so-called villains, his heart was in the right place.

'That man was not a serious criminal, but there is a real naughty one whose ten-year-old rescue Rottweiler was brought here twice in two months earlier this year. The dog was brought in when the owner was arrested for being drunk. He collected it when he was let out, but was then caught thieving, or something, and the dog was brought in again. The man was released on bail and the first place he came to was Battersea. He was banging on the door early in the morning, shouting: "Let me in. I want my dog." We were pleased to, because the Rottie was a real nasty piece of work and not able to be re-homed. I'm glad he did come to get the dog, because it was so temperamental and in such bad physical shape we would have had to put it to sleep. But I do wonder if he would keep coming back if he had to pay for him each time. I doubt it.'

A prisoner's dog has a card on its kennel door, which states 'PP' – for Prisoners' Property. There is another card, 'HP' – for Hospital Patient – because Battersea also cares for pets whose owners are unable to care for them due to their ill health. One little boy of nine with cancer arranged for his four Shih Tzus to be brought in while he went into hospital for treatment. He was in there a long time and when he finally came to collect the dogs they had been groomed. The little boy had been through so much and all he wanted to see were his dogs. When he saw them, looking so well, the delight on his face was very moving. He wrote 'thank you' cards to everyone involved at Battersea.

Kirsty is no softie; it takes a lot to make her cry. But she admits she wept unashamedly over an old man who had lost everything he owned in a house fire; everything, that is, except his two dogs.

Kirsty said: 'The old man saved his dogs, two bitches. They were brought in here, covered in soot, and he was taken to hospital. We settled them down and bathed them and put them on medication. But they had breathed in a lot of smoke and became very stressed and ill. They did not seem keen to go out for even a little walk round the yard, but they were so attached to each other that, if we managed to coax one up, the other would get up, too.

'After he left hospital, the old man went into a halfway house, to wait to be re-housed, and he would come here to see his dogs and let them know he was still around, and that they would soon be together again.

'But with just a week to go before he was due to move and get his life back, I had to tell him that one of his little girls wouldn't be going with him. She had kidney failure and there was nothing we could do for her. We needed his consent to put her to sleep.

'He just looked at me sadly, his eyes misting over, and said: "Can I spend some time with her?"

'I took him and the dogs to the new land near the arches on the north side of the Home and said he could stay there as long as he wanted. I went back an hour or so later with some treats and the dogs were running around after a ball the old man was throwing for them. They looked so happy, so pleased to be with him.

'I sat on the ground and chatted to him about his flat and everything, and watched him throwing the ball to the girls he had had since puppies. The sick little dog got tired and the old man picked her up and cuddled her. I got up and went back to my office, upset, wishing there was something I could do. It didn't seem fair. The old man had been in a fire and lost everything he had owned, but he had saved his lovely little dogs and now he was losing one of them.

'The old man was down there for hours, but then he came back with his dogs and said to me: "I'm ready now."

'I asked him if he wanted to be there, but he shook his head. "No, I don't want to," he said. "I trust you. I know it will be okay."

'I took his sick little dog and he led the other one down to the new land again for another run round while we did it. As I watched them walk away, I started to cry as it hit me what a lovely, caring old man he was and how he and his little dogs didn't deserve such rotten luck.'

If Battersea's staff had to cope with cases like that every day they would need Librium with their morning coffee. Happily, there are usually more smiles than tears in an average day, although the lazy or stupid attitude of some people to their pets does infuriate staff, particularly those in customer liaison, who are dealing with the public all day, every day, on the phone.

One of them Jayne Payne, who has been at Battersea for eight years, said: 'People would be shocked if they could listen to the abuse we get from some members of the public. The details of every dog we have here should be on computer and we check thoroughly when people ring up about lost dogs. If their dog isn't here, we always urge them to come to Battersea – ideally in the first seven days the dog has been missing – to have a look round for themselves, to put their minds at rest. Who knows, human error could mean

we've slipped up and their dog is here, but not showing on the computer. Around 70 per cent do come, but the rest make all sorts of excuses why they can't. We ask where they live, and give them the bus and train routes to the Home, but it seems they can't be bothered – they want us to save them the trip. Some of them have lived as near as Putney and still haven't come.

'I've lost count of the number of people who have given me the vaguest description of a dog and expected me to drop what I'm doing and go round the kennels to see if it's there. They don't seem to realize that there could be 200 dogs answering that description. We have to be masters in diplomacy, but it is difficult at times.

'When I tell people I can't possibly leave my desk, I often get a volley of foul-mouthed abuse before the phone goes down. It makes my blood boil and I'll go to the kitchen across the courtyard and have a good scream to get rid of the tension. It's important to me not to store up the anger, because the next person who comes on the phone will probably be calm and polite and perfectly reasonable.'

If an owner does go to Battersea and their dog is not there, they rarely go back. But some have, and between 1991 and 1994, when Tealby was used both for holding strays and as a sales block, people would come face to face with dogs they had lost. This would infuriate May Whammond, whose job was to escort the owners of lost dogs round Tealby. She would tell them their dog had been locked up unnecessarily for months and ask why they did not come back. Invariably, they looked sheepish and muttered: 'I didn't think it would be here.'

Some people, whose dogs have been re-homed, have the cheek to turn up at Battersea, thinking they have the right to see their pet again – in its new home.

May remembers, with some distaste, the woman who turned up last March, inquiring about a black Great Dane, called Boogie, a dog she claimed she lost *eight months* before. When May asked her why she had not contacted Battersea, the woman said she had been in the Philippines, but had phoned the Home every day.

'I knew that was a lie,' said May, 'because she would have had to give details of where she lost the dog and we would have matched it with the Dane on our computer. Then she kept changing her story. One minute she had lost the dog, the next her brother had brought it in – then it was something else. I got the truth by getting the woman to tell me her previous address and checking Boogie's details. I discovered that, according to the dog warden who had brought Boogie in, the woman had been evicted from her home in Wandsworth, south-west London, and had left the dog behind.

'I explained that Boogie was re-homed after a couple of months and she could not have him back. She asked for the new owner's

LEFT: White, fluffy and adorable … but how can the customer liaison staff know whose dog it is if the owner just phones?

47

address, but I told her we never gave out such information. We couldn't risk a previous owner going round to the dog's new home and, perhaps, kidnapping him or terrorizing the family. The woman seemed to accept that and left. But the next day she came back and I heard her asking another member of staff for the new owner's address.

'"Look, love," I said, as politely as I could, "you were told yesterday that we will not tell you that."

'"But I just want to know how my dog is getting on," she said.

'"Boogie is doing fine," I said. "He's happy in his new home."

'"How do you know?" she persisted.

'"Because we keep in touch," I said. "We sent a home visitor to the house to check on Boogie. And, by the way, he is not your dog any more." She whinged a bit more, then went out in a huff. I was glad to see the back of her, to be frank. If she cared about the dog, she would have found out where he had been taken and come to Battersea to claim him within seven days. After the police, this is the first port of call if you've lost your dog.'

For every person who cannot be bothered to go to Battersea, however, there are dozens who go back, week after week, month after month even, refusing to give up hope that they will be reunited with their beloved pet. There is one woman, in her sixties, named Maria, who has been going to Battersea every Wednesday for nine months, looking for her lost mongrel.

'She must have been here 40 times and we have got to know her so well, we don't ask to see her form any more,' said May. 'Since her dog disappeared, she has rescued a Retriever, which she is extremely proud of. But she misses her original dog and keeps coming to Battersea, hoping he'll turn up.'

At Battersea, all reunions are joyous occasions, but some owners have been known to get over-excited – to their cost. One West Indian, in his sixties, came in one afternoon, saying he had been walking the streets at night, looking for his dog, which had been missing for five days. He had not eaten for two days, through worry, and was close to exhaustion. When he saw his dog in one of the kennels, he collapsed with excitement and relief and May and another visitor had to carry him outside.

Unfortunately, the man did not have enough money for the claim fee, but May has the power to waive it in certain circumstances and she felt this was one.

'You only had to look at him and the dog together to see how much they loved each other,' she said. 'If I'm convinced someone is genuine and has not got the money, I will let them off the claim fee. But I can spot a phoney a mile off and they've got no chance of tricking me.'

May is not a tactile person; when a happy owner throws their arms round her for finding their dog, she is embarrassed and feels like pushing them away. But she adores seeing genuine caring owners reunited with their dogs and puts up with it, albeit reluctantly.

As Steve Lynn, Head of Kennels, so aptly puts it: 'Reunions never fail to bring a lump to the throat. It puts you on a high and makes everything we do worthwhile.'

Alex Martin, Kennel Supervisor, understands that as much as anyone. He went into Tealby one afternoon and saw an old man, in his eighties, looking somewhat distressed and confused. He said his Labrador had disappeared five days before. The old man had not brought his glasses with him, so Alex helped him fill in the necessary form, then took him to the first floor. The dog was not there, so they took the lift to the second. When the dog was not there either, the old man started to get upset. 'He ain't going to be here, is he?' he said.

Alex put his arm round his shoulder and said, gently: 'We've a way to go yet. We'll just carry on looking. You never know.'

They went round, looking in every kennel, but the dog was not in any of them.

'I don't want to lose him an' all,' the old man said, suddenly.

Alex looked at him, not understanding.

'I lost my wife three weeks ago,' the old man said. 'I don't want to lose him an' all.'

Alex felt his eyes filling up. He did not know what to say, just kept walking, praying they would find him.

They did. He was in the very last kennel – a gorgeous, portly golden Labrador, lying down, his deep, soft brown eyes looking at the bars, as if he knew the old man was coming for him. Seeing his dog, the old man broke down and started sobbing loudly. He bent down and put a hand into the kennel and the Labrador got up and licked it furiously. Overcome, Alex let himself out of a side door and stood in the yard, crying, while the old man talked to his dog.

Alex made arrangements for the dog to leave with the old man, then went with them through reception, on to Battersea Park Road, and hailed a cab.

'Thanks, boy,' the old man said to Alex. 'Thanks.' Then he got into the cab with the beloved old Labrador he had felt so sure he would never see again. With his precious dog sitting up beside him, he waved goodbye through the back window. He was still waving when Alex went back into the Home, tears streaming down his face.

There were some days, Alex felt, when he could not possibly be in a better job.

CHAPTER FOUR

Finding out what makes a dog tick

The old man's Labrador was one of the lucky ones; he was simply a well-loved lost dog, waiting for his owner to turn up. But for every dog collected during those first seven days, there are hundreds of unwanted, abandoned ones who face many weeks, often months, on the sales block in Kent Kennels before they are re-homed. The majority of such dogs are healthy and mentally sound and are put up for sale on the eighth day. But there are others, so traumatized by what has happened to them, that they have to be rehabilitated. And that takes time.

To find out which dogs are in good shape, and which are not, most of the staff get involved in assessing them – on the second, third, fifth and seventh days of the no-sale period. Reports are then written, so that the re-homing interviewers know as much about the dog as possible to ensure it finds a suitable home. Some of the dogs are very stressed, particularly the older ones, who have lived in a house with a family. Others are just plain nervous and cannot stop shaking. All are bewildered at suddenly finding themselves in a strange place, surrounded by people they have never seen before.

To be fair to each dog, two kennel staff assess at a time and they are changed during the course of the four assessments. By the end of the week, a dog may have been studied by half a dozen staff. This is vital, because a dog is likely to behave differently with different people. Also its behaviour might change over a few days, the more settled and confident it becomes: often a dog trembling with fear on day two has become a cocky, dominant animal by the end of the week.

Assessing begins in the kennel: is the dog confident or frightened of being approached by the kennel hand? It is then taken out and put through a thorough examination to see if it can be handled. The kennel hand will open the dog's mouth, touch its feet, look in its ears, roll the dog over onto its back, into the submissive position, to see how tolerant it is – and, very important, find out if it understands basic commands, such as: 'sit', 'stay' and 'down'. Kennel staff make notes of everything they see, so that their reports are as detailed as possible.

Re-homer Michelle Ritter said: 'We need to know so many things: is the dog dominant? Does it like to play? If so, does it like to play with people or just toys? Is the dog suitable to live with children? Does it nip or play-bite? Does it like grooming? Will the new owners be able to clip its nails, clean its ears? Is it food or toy possessive? Is it chase motivated? Is it going to run after joggers and nip their ankles? And, very important, how is it with other dogs? I'm trying to find out what makes the dog tick, to give it every chance of going to the right home.'

Claire Barnes said: 'When we're assessing, we want to find out as much about the dog as possible, so I'll play the role of a friendly person, with someone else acting nastily. It helps us establish what sort of treatment the dog has had, and what it responds to. Some dogs are so playful they don't mind who they play with. Others, which are more nervous and a little wary, are more choosy.

'To see how boisterous the dog is, we'll play with it, either with a ball or a squeaky toy, or roll around on the floor in the back aisles of Tealby.

All strays are confused at being in a strange place. Barking is one way they express their feelings and attract attention.

A HAPPY DOG

A happy dog is one that has a
home and is loved.

It is well trained and socialized
with people and animals.

It wags its tail and is eager
to please.

It has regular walks and
some toys.

It is not over stressed if it is left
on its own for short periods.

A happy dog likes being
handled and groomed.

Head of Rehab, Ann O'Brien, playing with
a new arrival to assess its temperament.

'Over the years, I've been extremely disappointed the way some assessments have worked out. I've seen one on the second day, and thought, "What a lovely calm dog – no problem there," only to find that, when it is assessed by someone else on the fifth day, it has found its feet and is a cocky so-and-so. It was probably a confident, dominant dog all along and was just insecure when it arrived.

'All the dogs are confused and nervous on that first day – unless you have a bomb-proof happy-go-lucky one that's just delighted to see anyone!

'The thrill for me is seeing a dog walk out of the Home into a new, hopefully happy, life and thinking: "I remember assessing you a month ago – you were a real pain and I was worried we'd never find a home for you." That's a lovely feeling. What I find hard to handle are the older dogs, who were lost or have been chucked out because they're not wanted any more.

'They may have lived in a lovely home for ten years or so, lying in front of the fire, or on someone's bed, and now they're in a kennel surrounded by dogs they've never seen before, dozens of them barking their heads off. It is so much harder for them to cope.'

For Ali Taylor, the Deputy Head Behaviourist, it is the 'latch-key' dogs – the ones pushed out of the door by uncaring owners and left to occupy themselves – that upset her, because she knows the chances of re-homing them are small.

'These dogs don't know anything about being important and relaxing in a family atmosphere,' she said. 'We do our best to re-home them as pets, but, to be honest, most haven't a clue how to behave. We can't expect them to settle into a home environment when all they know is the law of the streets.'

Assessment takes as long as necessary: puppies, of course, are usually quicker. A well-socialized puppy, which comes bouncing in and is interested in everything, can take as little as 10 minutes; another one that sits at the back of the kennel, shaking, can take half an hour.

With older dogs, it takes longer: not only are the behaviour and personality traits deeper, but coming to Battersea from a home environment is a shock to the

dog's system and many are nervous. Unless the dog has been brought in as a gift, the assessors will not know about its background, but they will be able to build up a picture of its temperament. If, for example, a dog is obsessed with people, rather than food or toys, this will be vitally important in re-homing it, because there could be problems for the new owner if the dog is left on its own.

Newly acquired land at the rear of the Home, in the shadow of Battersea's famous power station, provides the ideal space for assessments.

A dog with a compulsion to dominate is a big problem: this can really build up until the dog makes an issue out of everything and is confrontational all the time. An even bigger worry, however, is the dog with a vicious, aggressive streak that will attack another dog without weighing it up first, no matter whether it is male or female.

Head Behaviourist Jackie Donaghy said: 'There are so many people around these days who can't wait to complain about aggressive dogs that an owner can have massive problems – not only from the public, but the police as well. It is a big issue and, most of the time, the aggressive dog ends up being destroyed in case it attacks and bites a person.'

Clearly, no assessment can be 100 per cent reliable: for many unknown reasons, a dog's aggressive temperament may stay hidden and undetected,

only to surface later. This can have terrible consequences – as Lisa Wrobel, a Kennel Hand, discovered when she took a sick Greyhound, called Timber, from the treatment block back to his own kennel for the night.

As Lisa opened the kennel, Timber jumped on his bed. She closed the door behind her, then told the dog to get down, so she could re-arrange his blankets. But Timber just leapt at her and grabbed the back of her head. Lisa twisted to get away and head-butted the wall. Too terrified to move, she just stood there, facing the wall, the dog's teeth clenched on her neck. Slowly, she moved an arm towards the bolt of the kennel door, but Timber growled and grabbed it. He did let go, but Lisa was still trapped. She slowly opened the door and inched her way out.

'How I got out of that situation remains a mystery,' she said. 'I can't recall much except my fear. What I do remember is collapsing in the aisle outside the kennel – and all the other girls laughing.

'Timber reacting like that to me meant he was not saleable, so he had to be re-assessed. He was given a thorough going-over and eventually appeared well enough for re-homing. But when a nurse on the sales block tried to give him a tablet, he grabbed her arm and trapped her in the kennel. Another nurse eventually coaxed him to let go by offering food.

'Sadly, that was the end for poor Timber. He was given the benefit of the doubt with me, but had gone on to attack someone else, so there was no way at all that we could take a chance on re-homing him and he was put to sleep.'

Jackie Donaghy, too, knows to her cost how aggressive dogs can suddenly turn on people: she was attacked by a German Shepherd while cleaning its kennel four years ago, and was so petrified she feared she would have to quit her job.

'He kept staring at me, then grabbed me from behind, his paws round my waist,' she said. 'I kept pushing him down, saying "Get off, you randy dog. Don't do that!" As if in slow motion, the dog bared its teeth and then flew at me. All I remember thinking, in that split second, was my brother telling me that if a dog jumps at you, with its feet off the ground, try to grab its collar – so I did. Somehow, I turned him round and held him against the kennel door and brought my knee up to hold the weight.

'Other girls heard my screams and came running. They told me to move the dog along, so that they could get in. But I was stuck, too terrified to move. My thumb was locked in the dog's collar and I didn't dare let go, or move, because he was snarling and trying to get to me. I thought of risking a bite, so I could get out, but I was rooted to the spot, quite rigid, unable to do anything.

'It was only a couple of minutes, but I seemed to be stuck against that door for years! Finally, I managed to get the dog on to the ground, and one of the girls – newer to the job than me – dived into the kennel and grabbed it.

LEFT: Cleared for sale. It is now up to this soulful stray to charm himself into a new home.

BEHAVIOURAL PROBLEMS

If there's a problem, nip it in the bud at the first sign.

Stop and think, and look at what your dog is doing. Is there a signal that it is not happy?

Continue to reward good behaviour and ignore bad behaviour.

Exercise your dog's mind with mental stimulation.

Share the special tasks among the family, i.e. feeding, exercise, playing and grooming. Your dog should not rely on, and bond with, just one person in the family.

Ignore attention-seeking behaviour. Give attention when you want to.

Teach your dog some new tricks in order to gain control over it.

Changing or modifying behaviour should be done in a calm and controlled manner.

Be patient. Behaviour might get worse before it gets better.

Seek help if a problem persists. Read up on behaviour and if necessary consult your vet.

'I got away with a bruise, but she was taken to hospital with two massive puncture wounds. The dog walked off, eyes glazed, wagging its tail!

'I didn't know what to do for the best. I wasn't keen to go into another kennel, but felt that, if I went home, I'd never come back. I convinced myself the incident was a one-off and, half an hour later, went into another kennel, where two tiny terriers were on a bed I had to clean. "Excuse me, kids," I said, bravely, and reached for their blanket.

'One of the dogs bared its teeth and growled menacingly. I didn't wait one second. I ran out of that kennel and fled. I was found in a corner at the far end of the block, screaming.'

Somehow, Jackie recovered from that traumatic experience and grew to love German Shepherds with what she calls 'attitude' problems. Now, she does a lot of work with them for the Army and RAF and, ironically, is often the only one they allow in their kennels! This is all due to what she has learned from dog behaviour courses she has attended over the past five years.

'If I had a similar experience now, we would step back from it and would be looking into what was happening in the dog's life and why he acted the way he did,' she said.

Sadly, the German Shepherd that attacked Jackie was also considered too aggressive to be re-homed and was put to sleep the following morning. It is not something that happens often. A dog with temperament problems is now given a chance to see whether it would be fair to ask a new owner to take the dog on. It is sent upstairs to what Battersea calls its Rehab Unit, where an engaging young Irish woman, Ann O'Brien, and her staff look deeper into its assessment report.

The dog is given a three-week programme to find out whether it is redeemable and can be re-homed: the first week is spent letting the dog settle in and bond with one of the Rehab staff, who study the extent of its problems; in the second and third weeks work is done on those problems and changes made if the course of action is not working. By the fourth week, the staff know whether the dog is going to be responsive and, if so, how long it is likely to take.

There are up to 35 dogs on Rehab: some are lucky enough to be walked in Battersea Park by members of the public for more than an hour a day; others are taken to Battersea's new land for a 15 or 20-minute run around. Two-thirds of dogs make it through Rehab which means, for Ann O'Brien, the job has its highs and its lows.

'Battersea is an emotional and unique place, and one does get hooked on it,' she said. 'A high is working with a dog an assessor felt had no chance, then seeing it improve and walk out of here with a new owner you know is right. It's a feeling I find hard to describe – just warm and wonderful. A low is working with a dog that isn't improving, which, in the end has to be put to sleep.'

For many months, Ann feared that was the fate that faced a huge white Shepherd called Crachan, which paced backwards and forwards in his kennel on the Rehab Unit, like a wild animal. He was so vicious, it had once taken two hours to get him out for a medical check-up. Ann and a colleague had spent many hours trying to socialize Crachan, but he had been a guard dog all his life, and had little time for people, or other dogs.

Deep down, Ann knew she should not have put so much work into the dog and hung on to him; he was about six – quite old for a Shepherd – and clearly not re-homable. But her heart had ruled her head, and now she was stuck with him. One morning, she was looking at Crachan, wondering, as usual, what would become of him, when Duncan Green asked to see her. The company which had built Kent Kennels had been in touch, saying their guard dog had died. Did Battersea have a dog, unsuitable to be re-homed, that could come and work for them?

Ann felt like cheering.

The following day, a home visitor had a look at the firm's premises and reported that they could not be more ideal: Crachan would be given freedom to roam around a yard, doing what he liked. Just as he had done in his pre-Battersea life.

There are a couple of significant changes in Crachan's life today, however; he has become so popular that the firm's drivers come in every Monday morning with bones from their Sunday joints. And, by way of a 'thank you', the once-vicious 'wild animal' will sit still for the drivers to groom his thick woolly coat.

'He's in brilliant condition and everyone at Battersea is thrilled that he's fallen on his paws,' said Ann. 'Mind you, I bet he frightens the life out of passers-by when it suits him.'

Being taken out of its kennel for a walk is obviously the best tonic for a Battersea dog. The staff do their best to exercise as many as possible – including those on Rehab – but pressure of work prevents them from taking as many out as they would like. Now, however, they have a much-valued back-up – from the public.

The idea of dogs being walked by people not working at Battersea was not new when Nichola Vickers became manager in 1994, but it was not utilized. One reason was that

OVERLEAF: One of the Volunteers, Carolyn Amhurst, in Battersea Park. 'Walking dogs is like a drug to me,' she says.

no one had looked closely enough into the question of insurance and it was assumed the Home would not be covered; the other was the fear that someone walking a dog might not bring it back, having sold it, or kept it themselves.

Nichola, however, could see solutions to both problems. She looked into the insurance question and discovered the Home *would* be covered; and she saw no reason why dogs could not be walked for a limited time – provided she made sure they were the right dogs and the right people. Certainly it was something the Home needed: to walk every dog there for 20 minutes would take 10 staff 120 hours – obviously not feasible. So, Nichola started a dog-walking scheme she called the 'Volunteers'. She did all the interviewing herself: she studied cvs closely, checked the backgrounds of the interviewees and their motives, and carefully watched their reactions while being shown round the Home. If, at the end of a tough grilling, Nichola was happy, the Volunteer was taken on. If she wasn't, they weren't. So far, Nichola is delighted to report, the scheme has worked brilliantly. In the first year, there were 15 Volunteers. Now, there are 50. And while there has been the odd drama, no dog has been stolen, run over or involved in anything other than sorting out differences of opinion with other dogs.

One of Nichola's early volunteers was Carolyn Amhurst, a woman in her forties, whose lifestyle prevents her owning a dog herself. Carolyn has never forgotten being told, on her first day, that Greyhounds need walking most, and for the past three years she has exercised a number of them – often two at a time – between midday and 2.30 pm or 3.00 pm, virtually every day.

'I walk about a dozen dogs in a week – it's like a drug to me,' Carolyn admits. 'Some people go to church, some people love cigarettes but, for me, it is the dogs. Once I've walked three or four of them over a couple of hours or so, I feel good for the rest of the day. I'd rather do this than work out in a health club; it's far more satisfying. To me, looking at the dogs is like looking at a work of art: for the time I'm with them, I'm completely 100 per cent focused. For this reason, I always walk on my own, never with a group. I feel that if you're seriously interested in dogs, you shouldn't really walk with others.

'I feel sorry for the Greyhounds because most have been dumped when they are no longer useful. They have never really known any life as a pet in a warm, happy home environment. It seems awful to me that, in their last years, they should have to be confined to a kennel without even any exercise.

'I walk Lurchers, too, and they're quite similar to Greyhounds: they're not yappy dogs, who go mad the moment they see you. Even if I walked one just twice, it will spot me the moment I'm inside the block and strain to look at me. It won't jump up, it will just look at me, with mournful eyes, as if to say: "Are you taking me out today?" Lurchers and Greyhounds are so trusting.

They don't ask for anything. They're on my mind a lot, even when I'm on holiday. I'll wake up in the middle of the night, thinking about them.'

Being a Volunteer may be therapeutic, but it is not without its dangers, as Carolyn found out one August afternoon two years ago. She was walking a Greyhound on an extension lead in Battersea Park when it suddenly charged forward. Part of the lead was wrapped round Carolyn's forefinger and as she tried to hold on to the dog, it pulled taut, causing her excruciating pain. Such is Carolyn's love for Battersea's dogs, she made sure a passing member of the public took the Greyhound back to the Home before she was taken to hospital.

The first Nichola knew of Carolyn's ordeal was when she was returning from walking her own dog and saw a stranger bringing the Greyhound into the Home. For the next hour, she rang various London hospitals before tracking Carolyn down to the Charing Cross Hospital and going there immediately.

'It was a very scary time for her – and for us,' said Nichola. 'Carolyn's finger was not a pretty sight. It says everything about her that, even though she was in agony in the park, she made sure the dog was safe before thinking of herself.'

Over the next few months, Carolyn had to have three operations, but, unlike her finger, Carolyn's confidence was undamaged: she was soon back in the park, walking not one, but two Greyhounds – black and white brothers, named Max and Reg. What happened, however, nearly put her off dog-walking for life: Reg attacked a much smaller dog with such ferocity, Carolyn was terrified he had killed it.

She said: 'I'd let the dogs off their leads in a fenced-off enclosure when Reg spotted a little black bundle on the other side. Without any warning, he suddenly leapt over and tore into it. There was the most terrible screaming and yelling and I realized, to my horror, that the bundle was a dog. The owner, a woman in her twenties, was standing nearby, in a state of shock, powerless to do anything.

'I couldn't get over the fence, so I quickly put Max on his lead and hurried round. A man had gone to try to pull Reg off and he glared at me as though I was muck. He assumed the dogs were mine and I had no control. Who could blame him?

'The little dog was lying on the ground, not moving, just howling. The owner was shaking – like me. I thought, "My God – is the dog going to die?" I quickly put Reg on his lead and the lady gently picked up her dog. I apologized, and explained where the dogs came from, and insisted we went back to the Home, so that the vet could look at her dog.

'Reg could easily have broken the dog's neck, but, amazingly, it had no injuries. I was told Reg did not intend to harm the dog – he was just sort of playing. It is the Greyhound instinct, apparently: when they get out, after being cooped up in a kennel month after month, everything is terribly exciting, and they forget themselves and go rushing off.

'The owner calmed down surprisingly quickly and was very understanding when she knew the circumstances. I finally stopped trembling, but the incident really shook me up. If that little dog had died, I know I'd have had to give up being a Volunteer.'

Ironically, Carolyn's love of dogs led to an unfortunate incident at Battersea that has made her think carefully before being too kind-hearted – particularly where innocent-looking children are concerned. She came in one Saturday morning, just before midday, to find the reception area packed and staff under more pressure than usual. Two small boys, aged about 11 or 12, were standing around, looking lost and confused, and Carolyn's heart went out to them. Aware that children had to be accompanied by an adult, she asked them if they would like her to show them round and the boys said they would.

'I felt sorry for them,' Carolyn said. 'I assumed they wanted a dog, and would come back with their Mums or Dads if they saw ones they liked. They were particularly interested in Lurchers and Greyhounds and asked how much they cost. After about 20 minutes or so, they suddenly said they had to be somewhere and scuttled off, thanking me for showing them round. I watched them running towards the main gate, then went to collect the dogs I was due to walk.'

Carolyn did not give the boys another thought until the next morning when she was asked to go to the Home because a Greyhound and a Lurcher had been stolen and two boys had been caught on a security video camera. They were the same two boys Carolyn had taken round. The video showed them dropping the dogs over a wall, on to some waste ground next to the railway line, then climbing over themselves. Happily, the Lurcher was found the next day and brought back to Battersea. But the Greyhound – one of two sisters – is still missing.

Another Volunteer is Carl King, a train driver, who fell in love with Battersea after hitting a Rottweiler-German Shepherd bitch. Carl was driving his train on the Barking-Gospel Oak line, in east London, when he came round a bend and saw the dog in front of him. He braked immediately, but hit her at about five miles an hour. The woman driver of a train travelling the opposite way stopped and reversed Carl's train, so he could get to the dog. Carl was horrified to see that one of her back legs was virtually severed. Carl bundled the dog into his train and drove to the next station, South Tottenham, where he was met by an RSPCA team, who took the dog to their Handsworth Animal Hospital. Carl continued driving, with his shirt soaked in the poor creature's blood.

A few days later, Carl traced the dog to Battersea and he was invited to visit. He learned that, despite having her injured leg amputated – and damaged tail cut off – the dog was in good spirits. The staff had named her Network, for obvious reasons, and she was well enough to be put up for re-homing. Carl was so impressed by what he saw at Battersea that he offered his services as a Volunteer and now heads for the Home as soon as he finishes work. If he is on the night shift, he arrives at Battersea around 8.00 am and walks until 11.00 am; if he finishes at lunchtime, he will walk for most of the afternoon.

Carl, who is 29 and comes from Chadwell Heath, in Essex, says: 'If I'm honest, I've always loved dogs more than people and I'd love one of my own. But I'm sometimes out of my home 14 hours a day and it wouldn't be fair. Walking Battersea's dogs is the next best thing. They're all lovely – just like the people who work there.'

Happily, Network was re-homed quickly and has settled in well with her new owners – but the news is not so bright for people who get on Carl's train without their dog on a lead. They get a public ticking off from the driver over the tannoy system!

Nichola's volunteer scheme has been so successful it attracts people from all walks of life – from Brian Sheldrake, a retired milkman, to Katharine Hood, a dynamic businesswoman who gives not only her time to the dogs, but her computer expertise to the Home in general.

Sometimes, a dog's emotional state is simply down to its environment. Despite special attention in Rehab, or exercise with staff or Volunteers outside the Home, being cooped up in a kennel surrounded by equally miserable dogs barking incessantly, is the key reason for their unacceptable behaviour. If staff see dogs developing problems that reduce their chances of being re-homed, they step in. To give them another chance, they need to be transported out of the noisy, claustrophobia of Battersea and given some space and peaceful tranquillity – and a breath of fresh country air.

Happily they have that chance. It is called Bell Mead.

Bell Mead is seven acres of sprawling grassland surrounding a magnificent country house, built for one of Queen Victoria's relatives, less than three miles from where King John signed the Magna Carta at Runnymede, in Berkshire.

When the Dogs' Home bought Bell Mead 20 years ago, it had a world-famous reputation as a kennel staff training college, and Battersea's Committee wanted it to supply trained staff on a regular basis. But it did not work out that way. Most of the youngsters trained in the quiet English countryside were only 17 or 18 when they finished – too young for the hurly-burly of the capital. So, instead, the forward-thinking Committee decided to expand Bell Mead into an 'overflow' annexe, keeping the staff training facilities, but building more kennels for the dogs Battersea had no room for, and setting up a re-homing operation, similar to the one at Battersea. It was an inspired move that, over the past 20 years, has enhanced the quality of life for hundreds of dogs and found homes for many hundreds more.

June Haynes, a Kennel Hand, who nursed the dog through severe bronchitis, explained: 'Blackie came here as a stray in 1970 and was like my shadow. He'd follow me around the Home all day, every day. I'm sure he thought he was working, too, because he'd sit outside the kennel I was cleaning, as if to say, "Don't you dare come out till you've finished!"

'He was an intelligent dog – and a lusty one. If a bitch was in season, you could guarantee Blackie would find her. He'd jump out of his kennel and one of the staff would find him in hers. We put wire netting on top of the kennel, but he still tried to get out and twice cut his leg very badly.

'We re-homed Blackie three times, but he escaped each time and found his way back. We thought it was because he liked the quality of bitches at Battersea, but it was simply that he'd become attached to me and missed me. I desperately wanted to take him permanently, but my home was not suitable at the time. Finally, it was agreed that Blackie could stay at the Home as a yard dog provided he was neutered. That was in 1976 and Blackie enjoyed ten more happy years living at the Home, wearing a second-hand Harrods' coat, before he died.'

When Jimmy, a Shepherd-cross, arrived at Battersea as a stray, only a few months old, he was so thin, he was nicknamed Slim Jim. It did not take the staff long to fatten him up and fall in love with him. Sadly, one of Jimmy's back legs went wobbly and he wanted to lie down most of the time. The leg was X-rayed, but the vet could see nothing wrong. The staff decided he should not be put up for sale and he was promoted to yard dog.

David Cavill and his wife, Angela, who have increased Bell Mead's re-homing successes from under 20 to around 100 a month.

Nine years' later, Jimmy's lameness suddenly got worse. And then the other leg failed him. Jimmy could not balance himself; he looked as though he had mad cow disease. Finally, he was suffering so much he was put to sleep.

Thousands of mongrels have passed through Battersea's gates, but those two dogs will always have a special place in its history and in the hearts of the people who have worked there. Another, of course, is Racoon, the Labrador yard dog, who cheekily gave Nichola Vickers the once-over when she was interviewing staff. Racoon seemed convinced it was his job to let everyone know when the Home was shut: every evening, when the closing bell rang at 4.15 pm, Racoon would dash downstairs from the offices and belt up to the main gate, barking loudly.

ABOVE: Bell Mead's seven acres give Battersea's most needy dogs a breath of fresh country air – as well as another chance of being re-homed.

LEFT: Bell Mead supervisor Kay Elliott, with Sparky, the much-loved deaf Greyhound who broke the rules but touched the hearts of staff.

Racoon would settle down with the night staff, but one night he seemed irritable and kept getting off his bed and going out into the yard, barking. At 5.30 am he went out again, and collapsed. During the day, Steve Lynn looked after Racoon and when he came in at 9.00 am, a couple of staff took him to the dog and told him what had happened. Looking at the dog, dying on his bed, the two men got upset.

'You've got to realize he's getting on,' Steve said curtly. 'He's been here a long time. He's an old boy.'

When the staff left the room, Steve let out the tears he had kept under control. Then he closed his office door and sat with Racoon, stroking him gently, until he died half an hour later.

'I had kept a stiff upper lip in front of the others, but I was very upset to lose Racoon,' he said. 'He'd given longer service to the Home than I had.'

The most recent Battersea yard dog was a Rottweiler-cross called Desmond. When he arrived, in March 1996, and the staff were told he had been a guard dog, they were surprised. He was so huge, he *looked* the part, but there was not the merest hint of aggression in him: he shook nervously and seemed frightened of his own shadow; he was so terrified of people no one could imagine him attacking anyone.

The lack of aggression would have helped re-homing him, but Mel Wareham, Head of Re-Homing, felt it unwise to put him up for sale in case his 'scary' look attracted the wrong type of buyer. Also, she did not want to put him through another emotional trauma until he was calmer and more settled. In the end, Desmond was not put up for sale at all: everyone at the Home fell in love with him and, by general consent, he became *their* dog, spending every day taking it easy in Nichola Vickers's office with her own Battersea dog, Frankie. Soon Desmond's shaking stopped. He was more confident, and he seemed happy with his new life.

Earlier this year, however, Mel and Nichola were not so sure about Desmond. They started wondering: "Are we doing the best for him?" He *seemed* content. He adored Nichola and her secretary, and, particularly, Frankie – but when they went home in the evening, he was like a lost soul. He liked the night staff, but it was not the same.

Finally, it was felt that Desmond really ought to be in a permanent home, where he would be with people he loved, day and night. And, more important, where there was another dog. After much heart-searching, it was decided not to re-home Desmond from Battersea. Instead, he went on the TV programme *Pet Rescue* – and captivated viewers as he had the staff at Battersea. Normally, the Home receives between 300–500 enquiries from people wanting to re-home an animal featured on the programme. But Desmond was so appealing, he prompted 1300.

'The massive response fazed us a bit,' Mel admitted. 'But we were pleased, because it meant we were virtually certain of finding a suitable owner. It was unnecessary to phone all 1300 callers, but we rang a couple of hundred and found a married couple we felt were just right for Desmond. Ironically, they had a Battersea dog – a mongrel named Barney – which had had behavioural problems. They had dealt with those, which was encouraging.'

Wanting to be 100 per cent sure that Desmond was going to the right people in the right environment, Mel and Paul Wilkins, who works in reception, took Desmond to meet his prospective new owners at their home in Cambridge. They had a hunch the couple were perfect for him. They just hoped their home was. When they got there, they were overjoyed. The house was huge and so was the garden, and the couple even had part of a river as private property. Desmond took to Barney immediately, but not to his prospective owners; his nervousness of new people, sadly, was still there. But Mel felt the couple would help him overcome this quickly, and she and Paul returned with Desmond to Battersea, confident that they had found him what promised to be the perfect home.

The following week, shortly before Desmond was due to be collected, Mel sent a memo to staff, suggesting they staggered their goodbyes over a couple of days. She felt that by making a big deal of it on the actual day Desmond was leaving, he might be confused by all the kissing and hugging and crying, and get upset.

Desmond left Battersea in February and after his first night in Cambridge, Mel got a call from his new owners, saying that whatever problems the dog had had with people, he did not have them now.

'Apparently he slept on their bed all night and woke them up with a big, sloppy kiss in the morning,' said Mel. 'And he and Barney are playing all the time. They adore each other. We're all so thrilled for Desmond. He's living the life of Reilly. And why not?'

Battersea's attitude to Desmond typifies what the Home is about: no matter how much the staff love a dog, the animal's happiness and well-being always come before theirs; no matter how much they may love having the animals around them, the top priority is finding them new homes.

As Steve Lynn says: 'Kennels are far better for strays than fending for themselves on the streets, with the risk of being run over. In here, they get good food and treats, toys to play with, and they are talked to and bathed and groomed. But we can't provide all those little things – like a cuddle on the couch, a walk in the woods or a drive to the shops – that make life enjoyable and interesting for a dog; and give it that vitally important feeling of being part of a family and wanted by its owners.'

So, matching dogs with suitable owners is the perfect solution Battersea and

Bell Mead strive for – and, hopefully, the assessments provide information to help this happen. But there are cases where it is necessary to see how a dog reacts in a home environment before anyone can be sure it is re-homable. That's where Battersea's fostering system comes in: staff take these dogs home with them every night, either to socialize them with other pets they might have, or merely to re-introduce them to a family atmosphere. The fostering works exceedingly well, not only for the dedicated, caring animal-lovers, but for the dogs themselves: in most cases, they are so appreciative of the home comforts, they do not usually make it back to the kennels.

As Ann O'Brien says, wittily: 'When we take our work home with us, it usually stays there.'

LEFT: Crufts, a three-year-old Lurcher, was handed in at Bell Mead in March 1997. Sadly, a year later he was still looking for a home.

ABOVE: Desmond (left), whose TV appearance prompted 1300 enquiries, with Frankie, the girlfriend he had to leave behind.

CHAPTER FIVE

Homework to give a dog a chance

Ann is a good example of how fostering can help a dog. She took home not one, but three – and kept them all. The first was an adorable mongrel called Lir. Kennel life was affecting her so badly, she kept going round and round in circles. After a year, Jackie Donaghy felt she was going crazy and had to make a decision: it was not fair for the dog to stay in kennels, but it was not fair either to put her up for re-homing. Perhaps it was kinder to put her to sleep.

Ann, who had started at Battersea a few weeks after Lir was handed in, had become very attached to her and offered to foster her. Ann had had a lot of experience with dogs, but knew nothing then about behaviour problems and in no time wondered what she had let herself in for: Lir ran around in circles most of the time and even if Ann backed her into a corner, she would stand on her hind legs and circle. And she was so destructive, she could not be left on her own. She did not have the normal responses of a dog: she did not know how to play with toys and, because the only socializing she did was inside Battersea, she had a nervous aggression on the lead and was dominant with other dogs. Often, Ann felt she could not cope, and considered taking her back. But she stuck it out and, after eight months, started winning. Today, six years later, Lir will still circle when she is really excited, but she is a happy dog – never more so than when she is bossing other dogs Ann brings home for a brief fostering stay.

Ann's second dog was a Basset-Labrador cross, named Pie, who had been on the sales block for nine months. He went backwards and forwards to the pharmacy to be put on drips, because he was a physical wreck. But he is fine now. The third was Maurice – a Terrier-cross – who was re-homed three times before he was 12 weeks old, because he bit everyone who came near him. Battersea were not sure what to do with him, so Ann fostered him to give him a last chance.

She said: 'I had him for seven months and swore blind every day I was not going to keep him. He was a tricky customer – a rat on steroids – who bit me more times than any other dog I'd encountered.

'When I took him home to begin with he was so smart, he thought he was in control, not me, so I had to sort that out. At night, I'd get up every two hours and shift him out of the bed he was in and sit in it myself for three minutes before going back to bed. I was making the point: "I'm in charge, not you." And, in the end, I won. When I took him on, he was 10 steps ahead of me. We're just about even now! He comes to work with me and guards one of the grooming rooms.'

Kipper, a small, smooth-coated, black-and-tan crossbreed, had been in and out of Battersea three times in 18 months: he bit people in every home he went to, and everyone agreed it was not sensible to re-home him again. Everyone, that is, except Michelle Ritter. She said: 'I was not on a crusade, but he had been in kennels so long, I felt it would be a dreadful shame to put him to sleep without one more try. I may have a screw loose, but I found myself offering to foster Kipper to see if I could find out what the problem was. He flew at me within half an hour of arriving home on the first night – and, in the time I had him, he went for my flatmate twice. But I could see that he was a very sweet little dog, who didn't mean it. We did not think it wise to re-home him, however, and Jackie Donaghy took him on. He has calmed down now.'

Jackie has another dog, which she signed over to herself after fostering it. Mouse is her name, and when she was brought to Battersea, she was emaciated, bald and desperately unhappy. She was owned by a man, aged about 80, who had become so ill he could not leave the house to go shopping: he had reached a point where he was surviving on dog food. Then he had fallen over and was so badly hurt he could not move, and both he and Mouse did not eat anything for nearly two days.

Finally, someone realized there was a problem and arranged for the old man to go to hospital. Mouse was taken to Battersea, where Jackie agreed to care for her until her owner was well enough to have her back. When he had recovered, however, the old man did not feel he could cope with Mouse, so he agreed for Jackie to have her.

She told him that any time he felt he *could* cope, he had only to say, and she would hand Mouse back, but that never happened. The old man knows that his little friend is well loved and in caring hands. And Mouse knows it, too.

Ali Taylor has fostered three Chihuahuas – and kept them all. One, Ruby, died in 1996, aged 21, the other, Peggy, blind from birth, is still going strong at the same age, and the third, Pippin, has progressed from being a really naughty boy to doing obedience and agility classes with Ali.

'Pippin was a right little terror,' Ali said. 'He wouldn't let anyone touch him – not even his feet. I had him for four months, but didn't want to keep him.

WHY NOT HAVE A MONGREL?

Mongrels are hardier than most breeds.

They generally live longer because inherited breed traits are softened by mixed breeding.

They come in all shapes and sizes with a wide range of personalities.

Each mongrel is unique. You will not find another that is exactly the same in looks, temperament and character.

They are generally clever and very friendly.

73

I brought him back in the hope that Chihuahua Rescue would take him, but he was too big a problem for them. In the end, I kept him and persevered. He came through. He's a lovely boy. And very good!'

To Micky Swift, who works in Customer Liaison, the German Shepherd she took home from Battersea was the ideal dog for her. His name was Joey and she trusted him 100 per cent. When Micky had a baby, most of her family and friends advised her to get rid of the dog, but Micky would not hear of it. She took her baby home and laid him on the bed with Joey; the baby was the size of the dog's head. 'Here is your baby, Joey,' Micky said. 'You've got to look after him now.' From that moment, he did. He watched everyone who came to the house, and if Micky left the room where the baby was, Joey would go in there and sit. Watching and guarding him.

May Whammond is a sucker for old dogs. She has had five from Battersea but when one of them, a poodle, died, after just a month, the heartache was so bad, May told herself: "No more". But then she found herself on the second floor of Tealby looking at two cute Yorkies and the ugliest Pekinese she had ever seen – she had a badly overshot lower jaw, which made her fangs protrude up her face, giving her the look of a little devil. When May opened the kennel door and they all ran to her, the old familiar loving feeling started flooding back. She fought it, telling herself: 'No, no, no. They are oldies and you've got four at home.'

She meant to resist temptation, but the next morning, before she had even clocked in, she heard herself saying to Ali Taylor, who takes a special interest in elderly, small dogs: 'Those three oldies up there. What's happening to them?'

'We've got a home for the Yorkies, but not the Peke,' Ali told her.

'If you can't get one, will you consider me, please?' May said.

Ali smiled. 'All right, May.'

A day later, May was told she could have the Peke. Its name was Sam, but May thought the little dog was so ugly, she re-named it Uggy. Proudly she took her home to meet her niece and her poodles and spaniels.

Her niece was shocked. 'But you've got four dogs, May.'

'We're only fostering it,' May told her.

Over the next week, however, the girl noticed far more than a fleeting fondness in her aunt's affection for the new arrival.

'May, we're not fostering this dog, are we? We're the owners of the dog now, aren't we?'

'Yes,' May said. 'Yes, we are.'

Deep down, the tough little Scot knew she needed another lovable oldie to fill the space in her heart left by the poodle she adored.

With dogs of her own, Home Visitor Ann Challis

LEFT: Head behaviourist, Jackie Donaghy, with Mouse, a hospital patient's pet she took home for short-term fostering. Like many of these temporary arrangements, the dog became a permanent fixture.

has never been tempted to foster one from Battersea, but she did acquire one – by default.

Ann went to Battersea for a replacement dog for an elderly friend, whose Poodle had not long to live. A kennel hand showed her a Yorkie bitch, called Racoon, but Ann said no, because it looked too old. When the dog was let out of its kennel and danced around like a puppy, however, she fell in love with it. Ann took the dog home to look after it while her friend's kitchen was renovated.

Ann's husband, who has never been a doggie person and merely puts up with their Belgian Shepherds, was far from welcoming when he saw the new arrival.

'That's not stopping,' he told Ann.

'No, dear, it's going to Mrs Moore,' Ann reassured him.

But the dog never did. Like Ann, her husband fell in love with the adorable little creature. He re-named her Clover and soon would not go anywhere without her. When the time came to hand over the dog to her friend, Ann had to break the news that they could not bear to part with her. But she promised she would go to Battersea and buy her another, equally lovable, Yorkie – which she did.

Trixie, a Jack Russell-cross, had a home to go to but her new owners wanted her spayed before collecting her. Sadly, after the operation, Trixie went down with kennel cough and the sale was delayed. The dog got so bad that June Haynes took her home for the weekend. It was an anxious two days: Trixie refused to eat anything and kept vomiting. June fostered Trixie for five weeks, until she was better. But, by then, the prospective buyers had got fed up with waiting and had bought a dog somewhere else. June had a dilemma: continue to foster until another potential owner turned up, or put Trixie back in a kennel. Her heart took over.

'Trixie had got so used to me that it would have been like throwing her out if I brought her back,' she said. 'I couldn't do that. It would have been emotionally traumatic for her, I'm sure of that. So I kept her for another three months and, as no one wanted her, I took her on permanently. And I'm glad I did, because she's the most wonderful little creature. Mind you, she hates coming to work with me, even now. She had so many injections when she was ill, that she changes into a mad thing if we go anywhere near the pharmacy!'

Nichola Vickers did not want a dog. She was single and able to do what she liked, when she liked. She did not want a dog to change her lifestyle; nor did she want to be unfair to a dog. And then she saw Frankie, a light brown mongrel bitch puppy, which had been tied to a dustbin in Fulham, and suddenly everything changed.

Frankie, three months old, was horribly cut across her muzzle where elastic bands had been used to keep her mouth closed, her gums were badly damaged and her head was covered in scabs and scars. But she was a puppy with

personality, and when staff walked past her in the
treatment kennels, she would look at them appealingly,
her eyes imploring: 'Take me, take me, TAKE ME!'

'Head receptionist' Frankie enjoys a
lunchtime frolic in Battersea Park with
her owner, Nichola Vickers, the
Home's manager.

Frankie melted Nichola's heart and changed her mind.
The worries of leaving a dog on its own while she was at
work did not exist, because Frankie could go with her and do as she pleased.
That was two years ago. Since then, Frankie has been a welcome, lovable
addition to the people working under Nichola in Battersea's offices, and struck
up a wonderful, loving friendship with Desmond, the Rottweiler-cross yard dog,
before he was found a home.

For Nichola, the decision to have Frankie was one of the sweetest she has
ever made. 'I'd be lost without her – she's my best friend,' Nichola said. 'And
having a dog of my own is good for my job, too. It has helped me understand
what Battersea is really all about.'

For Frankie, the scars on her muzzle will never go, but the memories of the
pain she suffered in those early months have long been erased by the love she
is shown by Battersea's staff and the fuss she gets from every visitor she greets·
in her self-appointed role as head receptionist.

For Claire Barnes, the sight of Amber, a two-year-old Shepherd-Pointer cross,
was too much to bear: she was very ill with kennel cough and drastically underweight through not eating for four days. When the dog arrived at Battersea, she

WHY NOT HAVE
A GREYHOUND?

Greyhounds are often
misunderstood. They are very
affectionate.

Their love of company
means that some suffer from
separation anxiety.

They only need normal
amounts of exercise and will
happily relax all day on a
sofa after a 20-minute run.

They might look 'skinny'
but that is their normal
appearance.

They might enjoy a chase,
but not all of them do,
especially if they are
introduced to other
dogs properly.

They need a coat in cold
weather.

They make gentle, loyal and
sensitive pets.

was dreadfully behaved: she chewed everything she could get her teeth into, messed everywhere and howled for hours. But now she was ill, and subdued, and so sorry for herself that Claire's heart went out to her. She decided to take her home, to help her recover: instinct told her that when Amber was well she would be a fit and happy dog.

The good news is that Amber did get better. The bad news is that she reverted to her naughty ways, destroying anything that took her fancy. She even flooded Claire's dining room!

'It came as a huge shock to my Mum because she's always had Shih Tzus which never did anything wrong,' said Claire. 'She's with Amber all day and it's a big challenge for her. The dog is being destructive to get attention and Mum has to try to ignore her. She finds that hard, naturally. The problems are immense, but Amber has won our hearts. She fits in.'

Shirley Piotrowski had never owned a dog before, but she was taken with a scruffy, nervous Shih Tzu. The dog was a mass of tangled knots and stank of urine, but Shirley named her Molly, after the legendary Irish colleen, Molly Malone, and took her home. She quickly wondered whether she had made a mistake: the first night, Molly whimpered and cried into the early hours and, the next day, refused to eat or go for a walk; she just sat, chewing her blanket, crying. Shirley did not know what to do, but she was not going to admit defeat. She decided to take Molly to work and socialize her with other dogs. Sadly, that did not work either: Molly, neurotic and protective, growled at everyone who came into Shirley's office, then chased them down the stairs when they left, barking at their heels. When Battersea's then manager, Mr Wadham-Taylor, told Shirley to get rid of the dog, or else, she decided to leave Molly at home on her own. It was against everything Battersea advocated, but she had no option.

Shirley became interested in Shih Tzus. Every time one was brought into Battersea, she would make a point of having a look. She quickly discovered a common problem: they were all very smelly and looked as though they had not been groomed in years. Shirley made it her responsibility to try to re-home every Shih Tzu, and had her name registered with the Kennel Club, so that she could work as an official rescuer for the breed.

When Molly was eight, a Shih Tzu bitch arrived that particularly appealed to Shirley. It had been found wandering on Streatham Common and she thought it could be the perfect pal for Molly and took her home. When

Shirley got Milly home, however, Molly did not like the newcomer at all and Shirley would find herself being woken at three or four in the morning by the sound of the dogs fighting.

'One night,' she recalls, 'I fell on the floor and was wrestling with them, trying to force them apart. Molly had Milly by the throat and when I tried to prise her mouth open, she clamped her teeth round one of my fingers and wouldn't let go. Her teeth were only small, but the pain was awful and I was dreadfully upset. I didn't know what to do, but I was determined not to take Milly back; she didn't deserve that.'

A few weeks later, Shirley got a call from a woman in Peckham, south-east London, saying she was having to return a Shih Tzu she had bought from Battersea, because her son-in-law did not like it and refused to take the grand-children into the house while it was there.

Shirley took the dog home, much to Molly's disgust and her husband's dismay. Her intention was to foster the dog while a new owner was found, but when she came downstairs the next morning and found Milly and her new arrival snuggled up together in Milly's basket, Shirley suspected she might have a problem. She said: 'It was a wonderful sight and I thought: "Oh, how lovely – Milly has found a friend." I assured my husband I wasn't going to keep her, but he fell in love with her and insisted we did. I didn't need much persuading, I have to admit. We named her Mandy.

'Molly continued to beat up Milly for a while, but, gradually, Mandy came out of her shell and started to protect her friend. As Molly got older, the squab-bling became too much trouble for her and she just avoided them and went her own way. Sadly, she died two years ago, but I loved her to bits, despite her tem-perament and will never forget her. Milly and Mandy did, indeed, become the best of pals and I take them to work with me every day. They still love snuggling up together – usually on the sofa in my office!'

For more than three years, while Shirley was Duncan Green's personal assistant, she did re-home virtually all the Shih Tzus that came into Battersea – about 45 a year. If they had kennel cough, she would foster them until they were well enough to leave Battersea. One of the Shih Tzus she fostered was an unpredictable little horror named Toby. He went for her, and, while she was on holiday, he went for Duncan, who had taken over the fostering, temporarily.

'We had him for about a month and although he was a right little so-and-so, we all fell in love with him,' said Shirley, now Battersea's Special Events Co-ordinator. 'He was due to be put to sleep, but we couldn't let that happen, so I started looking around and tracked down a woman in south-east London who kept about 20 dogs. When I went in, I was overcome by the stink, and thought there was no way I could take Toby in there. But when I started talking to the woman and all her dogs came up, I changed my mind. She was lovely and so were they.

Jade Hall, who always sees the beauty beneath the fur of even the most forlorn of the Home's residents.

'The woman said she was moving to a big farm in Wales. That decided me: it was better that Toby went there with her than back to Battersea to be put to sleep. When I took Toby into the house, he was bewildered by the number of dogs. He was a cocky little dog and usually in control of every situation, but he just sat there, totally overwhelmed, while all the dogs sniffed him. I was worried and nervous and sad, and felt so sorry for him because he seemed so frightened. I wanted to rescue him and take him away with me, but I couldn't. So I left before I got too upset. The woman wrote to me to say that Toby had settled in well – once he had found his place in the pack. Not top dog at last!'

The joy Shirley felt reading that letter was tinged with more than a little relief: she had become so attached to Toby, she knew she would worry until she was told he was happy. It is an emotion shared by all Battersea staff who foster dogs, knowing that one day – all being well – they will have to put the animals' future in the hands of new owners.

Re-Homer Jade Hall, for example, found her first fostering experience heart-breaking. She took one look at Wren, the German Shepherd, and knew she had to do something. The dog was bald with alopecia. She was emaciated. She had mange. And she was going to be put to sleep. Jade went to Jackie Donaghy and said: 'I don't know why I'm here and I don't know what you're going to say and I don't know how we're going to deal with this, or what – but there is this German Shepherd and I really feel it shouldn't be put to sleep. I feel I can do something with her.'

Jade had never fostered before, but felt she could transform Wren and was prepared to give it a try.

'It proved a little embarrassing,' Jade said. 'I got some funny looks from neighbours who thought Wren's pitiful state was down to me.'

Happily, Jade turned Wren into the cracking-looking dog she felt she could be and she was re-homed quickly. Those miserable mangy days are now merely a memory. For Jade, it was a wrench giving up Wren, but her wonderful recovery and eventual re-homing gave her such satisfaction she has fostered nine dogs since then.

Hope was the name of the Rough Collie-cross, but hope was not something Battersea's vet, Shaun Opperman, gave her: what few teeth she had stuck out, she had bad breath and, more important, she had a heart murmur. She was getting on too, about ten, and Shaun felt it was, perhaps, unfair to re-home her. When Alex Martin asked to foster Hope with a view to finding a home with an elderly couple, however, Shaun agreed.

Alex was living with his partner, Lisa, a re-homer at Battersea, and they fell in love with Hope – so much so that Lisa would allow her to sit in the interview room while she talked to would-be owners. Nine days later, a woman in a wheel-chair came in, wanting to buy a dog. She could see nothing on the block she wanted – but, as she talked to Lisa, found herself becoming more and more attracted to Hope. She ended up taking her home that day.

Alex was amazed – and relieved. He said: 'I'd saved Hope's life, which was brilliant, but I was worried that I'd have to keep her, which would have been difficult, with both Lisa and I working. It was lovely when that old lady said Hope was perfect for her, but I must admit Lisa cried when she handed Hope over. That lovely dog, with the smelly breath and teeth that stuck out, was like our baby. We adored her.'

Not all fosterings have such happy endings, however. Tremble, a German Shepherd-cross, had to be put to sleep after two weeks with Ali Taylor, because she was just too nervous.

'Poor Tremble was not aggressive in any way – just plain scared,' said Ali. 'The only time she would be at ease was at night. In daylight, she was scared of her own shadow and once, in fact, charged through a glass cabinet, in fear at seeing her reflection. But, when it was dark and quiet, and all the lights were off, she would become confident and move around the house, checking things out.

'I put all I could into making Tremble feel secure, but I couldn't do anything for her. In the end, we decided she was such an unhappy dog it was cruel to keep trying to change her, so, reluctantly, we let her go. I was dreadfully upset, because it was so sad. All of us get upset when we lose a dog. If we didn't, we shouldn't be working here.'

Kennel Supervisor, Alex Martin: 'Sometimes I feel I've got the best job in the world.'

Ali has been at Battersea six years and will be there for many more. 'I'd feel guilty if I left,' she says, with a smile. 'I'd

81

be thinking: "Who's going to look after my little lost dogs? Who's looking after all those grey faces?"'

Steve Lynn liked the hefty, old Springer Spaniel about to be put up for sale: she was snooty and very pompous – a real character. But he was concerned she might go down with kennel cough – potentially serious in older dogs – so he fostered her, knowing she would hit it off with his own ageing Springer, who was deaf and slightly senile. Both dogs were going down the same road.

Steve named the new 'resident' Sally and took her to and from work every day. Sally was overweight, so, every lunchtime, Steve tried to exercise her. Sally preferred eating to playing and was far too lazy to chase after the ball Steve threw for her on the new land at the rear of the Home.

One lunchtime, four days later, Sally was sauntering snootily back to the offices for another dozy afternoon when suddenly she broke into a run, wrenching her lead out of Steve's hand. She ran towards the shop entrance to the Home, with Steve chasing her, fearing something had scared her and she was going to run into Battersea Park Road. But Sally was excited, not frightened. She had recognized her owner walking towards the sales block and, in the next few seconds was jumping up at her. The woman broke down and started crying and Sally was all over her face, licking her tears.

Steve said: 'The woman had been on holiday in India for three weeks. Sally was being looked after by a friend who had lost her a week before she was due home. For some reason, the friend hadn't thought to come to Battersea.

'When the woman saw her dog she couldn't believe it; she admitted she had not seen her with so much energy for years. She was so grateful, she wrote thanking me for all I had done, and enclosing a £100 donation for the Home.'

No one knew what had happened to make Foxy Lady such a nervous wreck, but one could guess. She had the most horrific burn blister on her back and was wary of everyone she met; she shook the whole time. Jackie Donaghy suggested to Steve Lynn that he fostered Foxy to see what she was like in a home environment. And Steve

Head of Kennels Steve Lynn and his two sociable dogs checking on a patient in the treatment block.

found out the first night what Foxy's problem was: she had a fear of kitchens.

Steve would feed his two dogs in the kitchen, but Foxy would not go in there. She seemed frightened even to pass by the kitchen on the way to the front door. Foxy loved playing with the other dogs, so Steve shut the kitchen door and let her chase a ball in the hall: she played happily, unaware the kitchen was there; and going to the front door was now no problem. Having gained Foxy's confidence, Steve opened the kitchen door and threw the ball in, hoping the dog would forget her fear and go after it. She did not do either.

Steve had been feeding Foxy in his living room, but now he started moving her bowl further and further up the hall until it was outside the kitchen door. Foxy ate unhurriedly. Her fear seemed to be fading. One evening, two months later, Steve threw one of Foxy's toys into the kitchen. She ran in after it, but suddenly stopped still, realizing where she was. Then she panicked and dashed out, leaving the toy there. Steve did not react, just carried on throwing her toy down the hall. After a few minutes, he threw it into the kitchen again and, this time, Foxy ran in, picked it up, and brought it back to Steve. He threw it in again and again and each time Foxy retrieved it, with no nervous reaction at all. That night, Foxy ate her dinner in the kitchen.

Foxy was the first dog Steve fostered. He had her for nearly five months and when she was re-homed – with a lovely family in Hertfordshire – he went to great lengths telling them what he had done to ensure that Foxy's fear of kitchens would never return.

Such is the importance Battersea places on people knowing all there is to know about the dog they are taking on, that it took him two hours with the prospective new owners. But it is not just Steve who is so thorough: all the staff are too devoted to the dogs, too dedicated to ensuring they go to suitable homes, to cut corners or take chances.

CHAPTER SIX

There's cats there too

Visitors to the Home are often astonished to discover that cats are very much part of the Dogs' Home Battersea. In fact cats have almost certainly been in the Home since it was founded in Holloway as the 'Temporary Home for Lost and Starving Dogs' in 1860. There are no formal records of cats being there at the start but, at a crucial meeting in 1881, John Colam, a committee member, raised the question of cats. Public attitude to cats at the time was that they existed exclusively to catch rodents, and if you fed a 'mouser' it would become lazy. There were certainly plenty of mice around in the 1880s, but obviously not enough to feed all the cats, who were often found dying from hunger and neglect. A major problem for the Home was the legal situation at the time. The law in London was clear that a member of the public could not take a stray dog off the streets because dogs were, and still are, classified as private property. But the police could. However, neither the public nor the police could take a cat off the streets because it was not 'goods or chattels', ie, it was not private property.

As Mr Colam explained to the committee:

'The law lays down certain provisions of relief through the police with respect to dogs, but in the case of cats there is no law enabling us to deal with them. Thousands of poor strays are found in our streets and squares. The police cannot take up cats, neither can private individuals, so that there is no legal way of getting a cat into the Home.'

Mr Colam came up with an ingenious solution to the legal problem. He carefully encouraged the Home to consider an activity he described as 'taking French law'.

'In these matters,' he said, 'perhaps a person may strain a point sometimes, and take the law into his own hands. But he better be careful how he does this.'

Money was raised and, in 1883, 210 cats were taken in. Two years later a new cattery was built. Since then many thousands of cats have been admitted to, and found new homes by, Battersea. At any one time there are around 80–100 cats in the Home with 15–20 available for re-homing, but thousands are cared for each year. The cats are kept separately from the dogs, and the activity of care, and finding homes for them, is quite different. Perhaps all they may have in common is that they are both Britain's favourite, and most domesticated, pets but occasionally in the swirl of everyday dramas inside the Home the lives of cats and dogs come together in a remarkable way. There is

one puppy named Muffet who is very glad he met a cat called Sophie.

In May 1998 a small Terrier-cross was brought to the Home as a medical emergency. She had recently been a Battersea dog but unknown to the Home, and the new owner, she was pregnant. She was having a very difficult birth because the first puppy had become stuck in the birth canal. It is possible that she had mated with a bigger dog. Shaun, the Battersea vet, had to perform a Caesarean. One puppy was already dead but everybody had their fingers crossed for the other five as staff tried to get the pups to suckle. Unfortunately the mother killed one of the puppies and it was clear that she had rejected the others.

It is often the case with Caesareans on dogs that because the mother did not experience the birth fully, and have a chance to lick and clean the pups, she does not recognize them as her own. Shaun explained that it was also possible that she may have associated her pain in birth with the puppies. He did not hold out much hope for the other four, one of which was very weak. Because their mother would not feed them, they would not be able to receive the crucial colostrum milk which contains vital antibodies, passed from mother to puppy. This milk is only available in the first 24 hours after birth and the pups are only able to absorb it for a short time.

There were no other dogs available who could adopt the puppies and hand-rearing of new-born puppies is surprisingly difficult. The pups have to be fed a

Walk into any office at Battersea and you're likely to see dogs or cats everywhere – even on the Director General's desk.

OVERLEAF: That loving feeling.

A HAPPY CAT

Cats are very self-reliant, but they want and need your company.

Spend quality time together and play with your cat, especially if you are out at work all day.

Stimulating toys such as food balls and scratching posts should be left for the cat while you are out.

Before going to work, hide some food around the home for the cat to find. Give it something to do.

If you have an 'indoor' cat, why not have two? They might not love each other, but they will appreciate the company.

Make sure the cat is wormed, vaccinated, that it has no fleas and is regularly groomed, especially if it is long haired.

milk substitute which initially has to be given every two or three hours, 24 hours a day. And sometimes the puppies may even inhale milk from the bottle which can lead to chest infections. Shaun had to admit that it would be surprising if any survived, but he was not going to give up. The veterinary team started the exhausting process of hand-rearing.

The branch of the Home at Bell Mead offered to help since they have 30 girls training as kennel hands, and a roster could be organized to feed the four puppies. They were taken to Bell Mead and, as soon as they arrived, the kennel hands tried to feed them from the bottle, but they would not take the milk. The situation looked hopeless but the Bell Mead staff wanted to try everything while the puppies, getting weaker by the hour, were still alive. They called one of their dog and cat 'foster parents' to see if they could help.

Nicky and Steve Frost, from Upper Halliford in Middlesex, came to collect two of the puppies to see if they could encourage them to feed at home with their four children, two cats, a litter of kittens, a Staffordshire Bull Terrier, an Iguana and a snake. Carly the Bull Terrier, warmly welcomed the two puppies, gently nuzzling and licking them. And even though they were still only 12 hours old, with their eyes closed, the two puppies were comforted by Carly and started to take milk from the bottle.

Nicky Frost was now faced with the daunting task of feeding them with a whelping formula milk every two to three hours. She had also fostered a cat called Sophie, who had a very young litter of kittens which were happily suckling and thriving. Nicky had a brainwave. What if she could get the puppies to feed from Sophie the cat, and could she persuade Sophie to accept the puppies? She took the kittens and rubbed their scent glands, which are on their faces, all over the puppies. When Sophie next went into her whelping box Nicky put the puppies and kittens in together. The maternal instinct in cats is very strong, but for a tense few seconds Sophie sniffed suspiciously at the pups. Then she settled back and they started to feed. The two pups were, from that moment, officially adopted and had a cat for a mother. Cat milk is obviously different from dog milk, so Nicky supplemented their diet from the bottle, but Sophie gave them much more than her milk. She gave them the warmth and the heartbeat they needed to feel secure.

The following day Nicky told the delighted staff at Bell Mead, and she fostered the other two puppies. Sophie had enough on her plate so the two new puppies were bottle-fed on whelping formula.

Unfortunately, after a few days, the weaker of the two puppies being fed by the cat, and the other two late arrivals, died. Nicky was heartbroken, but Shaun, at Battersea, reassured her that it was an incredible achievement that the one remaining puppy, now named Muffet, still suckled by the cat, survived and was getting stronger. When he was ten days old Muffet opened his eyes for the first time and must have been a little confused. One of the first things he saw in the world was the lens of a camera, and a BBC director who was there to record the historic moment. Whatever he made of that we will never know, but the next thing he saw was a group of very young kittens. Muffet immediately assumed that he was in fact a kitten. As he got older he rejected dog food, but loved eating cat food with his adopted family of kittens. When they played together he just could not understand why he could not manage to leap up onto the bed like the other kittens.

Sophie mothered Muffet until he was nine weeks old, then the Dogs' Home took him back to find a new home for him. Nicky Frost said she would never forget the little dog and she 'just hopes he goes to a home with dogs and cats and children.'

Muffet may be a dog who thinks he's a cat and perhaps, in some ways, he might be a bit luckier if he was indeed a cat. The Dogs' Home has very few problems re-homing their cats. In the last few years cats have overtaken dogs as Britain's most popular pet and, especially in big cities like London, cats are in some ways a much more likely pet to have. They obviously still need to be cared for, but they are much more self-reliant. They do not get lost very often and, if they do, it's sometimes because they have decided on a new home for themselves. The increase in the popularity of cats does mean that the trend in admissions to Battersea is increasing. In 1996 the Home took in 1454 cats. In 1997 the number increased to 2283.

There is still no law to clear cats from the streets, so that more than two-thirds of the cats in the Home are gifted to the Home by members of the public. This is usually because they are moving house or they have some kind of change of circumstance which means they can no longer keep their cats. A very common reason is that a new baby in the home is allergic to cats. Sometimes members of the public realize a cat is lost and bring it to Battersea. The police and other agencies very rarely bring cats in.

Once they arrive at the Dogs' Home the cats' futures are very bright. Some suffer a little stress but they do not display it in such obvious ways as a dog might. Usually a new cat will settle down to calmly consider, and choose, its next owner. Within three weeks 80 per cent of them are re-homed. The others may have to wait a little longer but, like the dogs, there is no time limit on how long they can stay at Battersea. Cats are only put to sleep if they are extremely

sick or old, or they are such feral cats that they can never be domesticated.

The staff find that cats are very easy to care for. They are 'smaller, quieter and cleaner'. But they do keep the vet quite busy. It is policy to neuter all unclaimed cats. Nichola Vickers, the Home's manager, is very straightforward about it.

'It is highly irresponsible not to have a cat neutered, unless of course you are keeping the cat deliberately for breeding. Because cats breed like rabbits.'

That's not as ridiculous as it sounds. Shaun, the Home's vet, strongly agrees about the importance of neutering cats.

'In some respects cats are like rabbits. They are induced ovulators, like rabbits, which means they have seasons, but mating is the stimulus for ovulating which makes them very fertile and incredibly prolific breeders. A pair of breeding cats can potentially be the head of a family tree of thousands of cats within a few years, if all their offspring breed freely. Also, neutering toms means they will not spray in people's houses, and there is evidence that neutered cats, male and female, live longer.'

Battersea is primarily a home for dogs and the staff are usually trained in the care of dogs. But as Nichola explains:

'We all talk about people either being "dog people" or "cat people", and most of the staff when they arrive at Battersea think of themselves as dog people. However as the weeks pass they become more and more fond of the cats. Sometimes the same process happens with members of the public who apply to have a dog, but wander around the cattery and are surprised with their own decision to take a cat.'

Very often members of staff just cannot resist some of the cats who come in. Christine Harvey has been a kennel hand for four years and, apart from working as a relief van driver, she is employed exclusively to look after the cats. Over the years she has not been able to resist some of the cats that the Home was having problems re-homing. One by one she has taken them home herself to keep, and now she has three of her own.

BELOW: Christine Harvey, with a feline friend. 'I still enjoy working with the dogs but I try to spend as much time as I can with the cats.'

LEFT: Two new arrivals.

'I just thought "I want these cats". So I took them home and kept them. Sometimes I think maybe I could take just another one. There are always cats coming in which make me feel like that. Cats are my main love. I really like advising people, when they come to buy a cat, which one would be best for them and what to do with it when they take it home. Working here I get to know the temperaments and characters of each of the cats and, especially if people have a small child, I like to help them decide on the right cat.'

June Haynes, another kennel hand, has worked at Battersea for 22 years and has also grown very fond of the cats.

'I do enjoy the cats. They are quite different from dogs. A cat came in recently called Karn, a great big black tom. The boy who brought him said you couldn't go anywhere near him or touch him. It took us weeks but we eventually got round him. He became really friendly and affectionate and has been re-homed. It was a real pleasure to work with him. You have to have patience with cats and let them come to you, to some extent. They are not difficult to re-home, and the cats are at Battersea for a much shorter time. With a cat the owner doesn't have to be with it all day, but we don't like giving cats to people who are out all the time. Even cats need company. At the weekend we get lots of working people who come to look for a cat to take home. I can understand why they want a pet. We recently had a lecture from an animal behaviourist and it seems everybody in London lives in flats.

'They have to have "indoor" cats, but sometimes an indoor cat becomes bored and destructive. They will go for the curtains, upholstery, floors and pot plants. People have to bear that in mind. But I know that a lot of the people who re-home cats from us are very happy with what they get.'

As with the dogs, the re-homing of cats is a skilful job of matchmaking which should leave both cat and new owner happy with each other. One of the aspects that has to be considered is the history of the cat before it came to Battersea: what it likes to eat, does it like being handled and, in particular, was it an 'indoor' or an 'outdoor' cat. Some people live in high-rise flats without gardens and their cat will have spent almost all of its life indoors. It will not have become streetwise and could have problems with a main road if it is allowed to come and go. On the other hand a cat used to being an 'outdoor' cat would suffer stress if kept indoors all the time. The staff try to ensure continuity in the cat's life, but sometimes it is not that simple. Occasionally an 'indoor' cat is gifted to the Home and its history reveals signs of obvious stress and boredom such as messing around the house, and ripping furniture. In cases like these, the re-homing staff will decide that the cat should be placed in a new 'outdoor' cat environment, with detailed instructions to the new owner to carefully introduce it into the outdoor world.

It is not unusual for staff to foster cats, especially if there is a problem.

Michelle Ritter, a re-homer, has developed a speciality; she takes very difficult cats home with her.

'I fostered Gizmo, a psychotic cat, and Cramble, who was a little bit feisty, and Toffee, who had an allergy round his neck. All have been sorted and re-homed.'

Cats, it seems, often decide for themselves who their new owner is going to be. Christine Harvey tells the story of a cat that jumped through the bedroom window of an unsuspecting man who lived on his own. While he was asleep she made herself a little bed in a wardrobe. The man had no idea she was there until two days later when he heard meowing coming from the wardrobe. He opened the door and found mum and four kittens. He took them to the Home and had already decided, since the cat had chosen him, that he would like to keep her. Battersea kept the mother with the kittens until they were nine weeks old. They were instantly re-homed and, since nobody reclaimed the mother, she went back to the home she had chosen for the birth of her kittens.

In one case, a cat decided that where it wanted to live was in the Dogs' Home itself. Several years ago a stray came over the wall from the gas works. Staff tried to catch her but she evaded all their attempts. She started to turn up every day for food and eventually she was captured and neutered. They named her Girly, and made a bed for her in the cat house, with a cat flap, so she could come and go as she pleased.

As Christine Harvey says: 'She is the Home's cat, and she is always around here. She's a tortie, that's a ginger-mix, and she is definitely one of my favourites. Every morning when you go in she is there meowing at you for some breakfast. No one has re-homed her and it's nice that she does what she wants. Because she keeps coming back you just know she is going to be there and she enjoys life as it is.'

Christine has always liked cats and sometimes she finds it hard to believe that it's actually her job to look after them.

'Some people might think it's an easy job, but it is hard work and there's a lot to it. But I am lucky, I love working here.'

As a relief van driver, Christine still enjoys working with the dogs, but there is one difference with the cats that she really appreciates.

'We don't get many ill-treated cats. A bit underweight or riddled with fleas is about as bad as it gets. Usually, with cats, the owners who gift them to us are genuine people with genuine reasons why they can't cope.'

A NEW CAT IN YOUR HOME

Don't leave a new kitten home alone for more than three hours a day.

For an 'indoor' kitten, make any balcony safe, i.e. by using wire mesh.

If it is an 'indoor' kitten, why not have two at once? Unless you already have a cat.

The cat should have access to a high area to escape to, especially if there are children in the house.

Confine the cat to one room for a couple of days. Introduce the rest of the house in stages.

Keep the cat in the house and seal any cat flaps for the first three or four weeks.

For the first time out, supervise the cat and miss out its morning meal. A hungry cat is more likely to come back.

Looking after cats at Battersea Dogs' Home is certainly going to be an expanding part of the job market. With the increasing popularity of cats, the Home is already dealing with increasing admissions and is preparing itself for the future. Duncan Green has no doubts about that.

Two more satisfied customers complete the purchase of the cat of their choice.

LEFT: Taking it easy at Bell Mead.

'We've taken in cats since 1883, and are more committed to their care than ever. With an expected rise in population, one of our next big projects is a state-of-the-art cattery, to match the range of facilities available for the dogs, with their own dedicated areas of care and expertise. Perhaps one day Battersea will be as well known for its cats as it is for the dogs.'

Duncan has never been short of ambitions for the Home. He has a twinkle in his eye when he adds, 'The Cats' Home, Battersea ... it rolls off the tongue.'

**INTRODUCING A NEW
DOG TO YOUR HOME**

Before you take a new dog into
your home, take it to the place
where you want it to relieve
itself regularly. Praise it when
it is finished.

Immediately establish the
dog's own bed area and put
an old jumper or something
with the smell of the owner
on it.

On the first night, settle it
down, leave it some water and
walk out of the room. Do not
return no matter how persistent
the whining.

Perhaps leave a radio on, set
to a talking station. A clock
with a loud tick is also good
for puppies.

On the first morning, if your
dog has made a mess, do not
scold her. Clean the mess out of
her sight – do not encourage
her to get attention
by messing.

Clean any mess with clothes
washing liquid or powder to
avoid residue smells for the
dog which might encourage
it to mess there again.

taught how to handle the public, diplomatically and rationally, in difficult, tense or emotional situations. Now, it is a case of: 'Let's find out why these people can have a dog.' And the letters of complaint are negligible.

Battersea's re-homers are male and female. Most are in their twenties; all are courteous, knowledgeable, and eager to help you find the dog you want, which will suit your lifestyle. All the re-homers know the dogs in Kent Kennels – particularly residents that have been there several months – and this often proves useful and time-saving for people who know the type they are looking for.

Steve Lynn, for instance, was interviewing a man with years of experience of Collies. He wanted another one – and Steve introduced him to Army, who had been on the sales block for two months. Steve had a hunch the two would hit if off – and they did. They walked out happily together, a perfect couple, just 40 minutes later.

Unlike that gentleman, most prospective buyers do not know what they are looking for, much less what is suitable. Many are grateful for any help or advice from the re-homers, who, in dealing with hundreds of would-be owners over the years, have learned to read people and get a feel for what might be appropriate. Unfortunately, some people have a preconceived idea of what they want and, often, do not react kindly when told they cannot have it. But it is a fact of Battersea life that the re-homers will not – under any circumstances – sanction the sale of any dog to any person if they are worried that one is not suitable for the other. What they are trying to achieve in each case is a perfect marriage between person and dog. And if they do not feel it is going to be perfect, the partnership does not go ahead.

At the end of your interview, you will be told that, on each kennel, there is a card – pink for girls, blue for boys – giving basic details about the dog, such as its age, how long it has been in Battersea, as well as brief information about the dog's character. The details describe how the dog gets on with children and pets, how it behaves when left on its own etc., as well as personality quirks, such as escapology. You are now ready to look at all the dogs Battersea has for sale. You will go through to a ramp, leading to the kennelling area, usually with the re-homer saying: 'Good luck. But try not to let your heart rule your head.' And advising

you to take several alternative cards, in case the first dog you choose proves unsuitable.

The reception area, like the staff waiting to interview you, is bright and welcoming. But you have to be patient; buying a dog to suit your lifestyle takes time.

There are 180 kennels on three floors and, for most visitors, the sight of so many dogs is overwhelming. Many people are shocked that they cannot see many pedigrees, and the staff are always being asked: 'Where are the Dalmatians, or Labradors, or Scotties?' But you'll find mainly crossbreeds at Battersea, predominantly German Shepherd, Greyhound and Border Collie mixtures.

Hundreds of people come to Battersea to rescue unwanted puppies and are surprised that none is for sale. The Home takes a stringent view on where puppies should spend the rest of their lives.

Many are rescued from puppy farms where they have been poorly treated. Others are dumped or abandoned by owners who did not realize just how much work they involved. Some are found wandering the streets in a horrendous physical state, and need nursing back to health. All are nervous, having been through a trauma. Most are terrified.

Occasionally, puppies are born in the Home. Many are in need of special

care because their mothers have been abandoned and are not well themselves. At Bell Mead, for example, a bitch died having a Caesarean: one of her puppies was black, with white paws that looked like gloves, so the staff named him Michael Jackson. Because the orphan pups needed hand-feeding every two hours, Michael went to stay in a foster home, but came back to Bell Mead because he became very poorly. He was nursed back to health, but now was found to be deaf. The staff now knew they were looking for a very special home for their precious boy.

A wonderful, caring couple came to Bell Mead and bought not only Michael but also a friend to be his ears – a middle-aged Staffie-cross. The dogs have obviously learned the art of sign language because, even a year on, they play non-stop and understand each other perfectly!

Understandably, Battersea's professional procedure is even more protective of these little waifs; under no circumstances do the staff want the puppy to have a second bad experience. Therefore, even more time is spent selecting suitable homes for these tiny charges. If you are willing to go through a very detailed interview and are prepared to wait in a long queue, you may be able to re-home a Battersea puppy.

BELOW: Some of Bell Mead's team, with their much-loved star, 'Michael Jackson' (centre), the one-time orphan puppy with 'white gloves' who had to learn sign language from his adopted sister.

LEFT: On their way to a new home and the start of a new life together.

The waiting and interviewing over, an excited little girl showers affection on a lovable dog that Battersea's expert re-homers feel is a suitable pet for her and her family.

Special dogs need special owners. What an accolade if you succeed!

If you see a dog whose details fit in with what has been discussed at your interview, you take the card from the front of the kennel and go downstairs to another interviewing area, called 'Taking Away', where another re-homer compares the notes on the card with those provided by the first interviewer. If the notes match, meaning the dog you have chosen is suitable, the re-homer will fetch the more detailed assessment notes and discuss everything known about the dog. If you still want to go ahead, the dog is brought to a meeting room for an introduction and you are encouraged to try to bond with it by play or by grooming – anything to determine whether there is a mutual affection. If the dog is confused about who it should be with, the re-homer will leave the room and watch what happens through a small window. Hopefully, the dog reacts well to you – and everyone you might have with you – and vice versa. If so, the dog is taken back to its kennel while the re-homer deals with the paperwork for the sale and organizes a medical check.

Dogs cost anything from £50, depending on size and whether or not they are a particular breed. In addition to the dog, a new, and always very excited and happy, owner is given leaflets advising on settling a dog in its new home, vaccinations and flea control, and a bag of food. Notes about the dog's diet while at Battersea are also provided. Before leaving, the dog will be given a microchip: it is the size of a grain of rice and is embedded into the scruff of the neck. The dog is given a green disc for its collar, which, in the event of it getting lost, explains that the owner can be located through a central computer by scanning the microchip.

That is the ideal scenario, the one where the dog and its proud new owners walk off happily together and the re-homer feels richly rewarded for arranging another – hopefully – perfect marriage. Unfortunately, many of the scenarios played out in Kent Kennels are less than ideal.

Being nationally famous, Battersea attracts thousands of people throughout the country who have decided to buy a dog. For all of them, it is a monumental decision that has taken weeks, maybe months, to reach – a decision that will dramatically transform their lives. When they walk into Battersea, it is the beginning of a hugely emotional experience, and the staff understand that: as devoted animal lovers and pet owners themselves, they appreciate, probably more than anyone, what a profound commitment taking on an animal is.

Sadly, for them, their understanding, and, more important, their knowledge and experience, is far too often thrown back in their faces by rude and obnoxious people, some of whom can be intimidating, even violent. As Mel Wareham says: 'Many people come here with a vision of walking away with a wonderfully cute, cuddly creature there and then. And they get upset when they realize it does not happen like that.'

While the staff are trying their hardest to achieve that perfect marriage, some prospective owners, who think they know better, stretch their tolerance by ignoring what they have been told and flouting Battersea's tried and tested policy. The biggest headache for re-homers is when prospective buyers do not bother to read the cards on the kennels or, if they do, ignore what they say, and choose a dog they know, from their first interview, is totally unsuitable.

Like all her colleagues, Jade Hall has been exasperated by some customers' stupidity or arrogance, or both.

She said: 'It's vitally important we don't let people's hearts rule their heads, so we spend a lot of time explaining why they should consider certain dogs and

A NEW DOG MEETS YOUR DOG

When selecting a new dog, think carefully about how the new dog might get on with your existing dog. If possible, introduce them before you choose your new dog.

Generally, the more different they are, the more likely they are to get on because they won't compete. Think about matching male with female (both neutered), old and young, big and small.

Introduce a new dog to your existing dog on neutral territory. They should meet for the first time outside the home.

At first, do not leave any of your old dog's toys lying around.

Until you are confident, the dogs should be supervised during feeding. Feed them well apart from each other.

If a family already has a dog, Battersea's re-homers will insist on it meeting the prospective new addition.

not others. I've lost count of the number of times people have come back down having chosen dogs totally different in type, size and temperament from what I've suggested. People will insist they want a dog that's house-trained and past the chewing stage, so I'll tell them there's a lovely three-year-old who's just perfect. Then they'll go up and see a year-old puppy and they say: "Oh, he's lovely – we want that one," and all the reasoning goes out the window.

'Others, with children, who I've warned to avoid certain dogs, come down having chosen one that is obviously not right, and argue with me: "He was lovely in the kennel," they'll say. "My kids touched him and he was fine with them." What they don't appreciate is that we have lived with that dog and know it will behave differently outside its kennel. It's likely to be mouthy and boisterous, and jump up and want to bite the children's noses.

'Many of the dogs at Battersea haven't had the best upbringing and training and will not be suitable for younger children because they haven't been disciplined. But many people don't understand that. Or don't want to.'

Claire Barnes who works on 'Taking Away' at weekends, gets annoyed with those people who place more importance on a dog's looks than its personality and temperament. She said: 'The card on the kennel will state clearly, "This dog is destructive. Not house-trained," but you wouldn't believe the number of people who say, "I don't care – I'll have it because it looks lovely." I have to ask them if they're prepared to have their home wrecked when the dog wets the carpets every day for weeks. My job is to make them think about what they're saying and doing. Often they respond well. Sometimes they don't.'

You don't have to want to buy a dog to visit Battersea. For 50 pence, you can spend half an hour looking around. Sometimes people doing just that fall in love with a dog and rush down to 'Taking Away' gleefully, thinking they can buy it on the spot. Obviously many are disappointed to be told that, not only do they have to go back to reception and wait to be interviewed, but they may then be told the dog they want is unsuitable for them. People who make this mistake are usually genuine, but Battersea's re-homers are used to tricksters who think nothing of lying to walk off with a dog.

When trying to clinch a purchase in 'Taking Away', for instance, a couple might deny what was agreed in the first interview. The second re-homer has the first one's notes, so there is no chance of dubious customers getting dogs they should not have. But that does not stop people from treating Battersea's staff as stupid and naive and trying to pull the wool over their eyes. In a first interview, someone might say the dog will live outside in a kennel but, having picked a huge dog, they will suddenly change that to a stable; from saying there are no children in the home, the person might let slip that her five grand-children visit every week!

Once, a wife's lies landed Battersea in the middle of a marital muddle. She turned up with her daughter and convinced a re-homer to sell them a dog on the basis that she was separated from her husband. But a few days later Nichola Vickers received an angry phone call from the husband, demanding Battersea took the dog back. 'My home is turning into a zoo,' he fumed. 'We've already got two dogs – and rabbits. The new dog is messing everywhere and I don't want it. Take it away.'

Two days later, the RSPCA in the area near the couple's home, rang Battersea, asking about the man in question. Apparently, he had dumped the new arrival in the middle of nowhere and it had been found wandering as a stray. The RSPCA believed it was done maliciously. The dog was returned to the couple's home, but the husband kept pestering Battersea to take it back. Nichola faced a dilemma: should she put the dog through the trauma of being brought back to a kennel? Or should she let it stay at the house, amid all the tensions of a marital dispute?

In the end, she arranged for Ann Challis to go to the house and try to sort it out. 'Ann is good in awkward situations and, if anyone could make them reach an amicable solution, she could,' said Nichola.

Ann found everything calm at the house – until the husband came in and started raising his voice, telling her how terrible the dog was. 'The dog must have heard it all before and began barking to protect his owner,' Ann said. 'It had every opportunity to bite the man, but didn't. He was a good dog and only doing his job.'

But the husband wanted the dog out of his life – put to sleep, preferably. He had been taking him out, goading him to bark, then tape-recording the noise to convince a court the dog was dangerous and threatening him. Ann reported back that it was the husband who was the problem, not the dog, and Battersea refused to take him back. As far as Nichola was concerned, the wife was a sensible dog owner and the animal was safe – and, with the dog, so was she. The couple needed to resolve their differences. Or get divorced.

Often, the lies are pathetically transparent. One weekend, last spring, a couple in their early twenties filled in a form to buy a dog, but found nothing that caught their eye. They saw someone leaving with a Staffordshire Bull Terrier – and decided that was the type they wanted. A re-homer told them there were some Staffs in Tealby, but people were allowed in that building only if they had lost a dog.

'But we have,' the man said quickly.

'So why did you fill out an interview form to buy a dog?' the re-homer asked.

The man made some excuse that he was confused by the system, and insisted he had lost a dog two weeks before.

'If you have only just lost a dog, I'm afraid we can't sell you another one,' the re-homer told him.

At this, the man became aggressive and demanded to be shown to where the lost dogs were kept. To pacify him, the re-homer arranged for Claire Barnes to take them round Tealby. But before they left, she jotted down a note saying what the couple were trying to do, and quietly gave it to Claire under the desk. The couple had completed a Lost Dog form, and Claire quickly realized that, because no such dog existed, they had had trouble answering the very specific questions. Claire asked them some more and the man got impatient. 'Look love,' he said, brusquely. 'Are you going to take us round or what?'

'I might take you round,' said Claire. 'Or I might just look up the dog's details on the computer.'

'I want to go round,' the man insisted.

Claire said it would be simpler and quicker to check the computer: the man was behaving in precisely the wrong way to buy a Battersea dog, and she was eager to get his name and address, so that he would never get one. To his annoyance, she checked the computer, then told him that no dog answering the

description they had given had been brought in during the past two weeks – or even two months. Angry at being thwarted, the man shouted at Claire, saying the whole place was 'bloody useless,' then stormed out, saying they had made a mistake going there.

Even such blatant liars are handled as tactfully as possible by the staff. But it is not always easy.

Jade says: 'We have to be assertive, really confident in what we're saying, because we have to convince people that we know what is best for them. I always try to find a dog for a person. If I can't, I say I'll keep the form and contact them if one comes in I think is suitable. The last thing we want is for people to go away, unhappy, thinking we are being unhelpful because, then, they'll just say: "Let's go to a pet shop and buy a puppy."

'I hate it when people are aloof and just answer "yes" or "no" to questions. You have to dig in and persist, but there are many who, for one reason or another, don't want to give anything away. I've had really obnoxious people who

Saying goodbye is bitter-sweet for the staff – the tearful moment when their hard work ends and the dog's new life begins.

OVERLEAF: All smiles as a happy Battersea resident gives a re-homer a farewell lick before leaving with its new owner.

If you want to
re-home a Dog or Cat
please take a ticket from
the reception desk and
fill in an application form
and wait for an interview

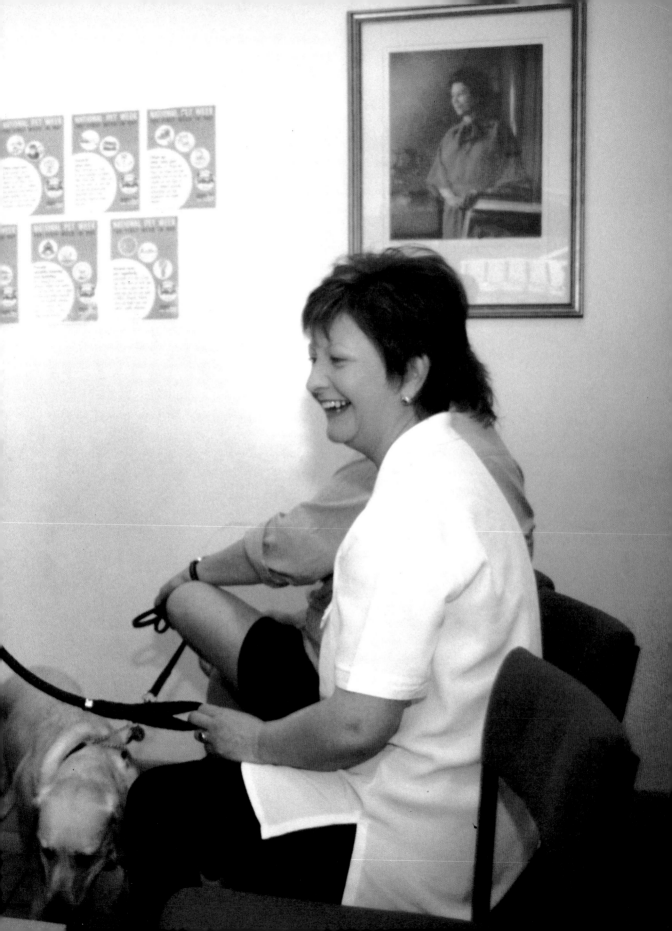

won't even look at me when I'm talking to them. I can understand that some people are nervous of coming in and being grilled – I know I would be! But with many, I get the impression that they take one look at me and think: "Young girl – what can she know?"

'My worst experience was earlier this year when I interviewed a woman in a wheelchair, on a very busy Saturday, who came in with her daughter and son-in-law. I could feel the tension building up and them getting angry as I asked one question after another and it dawned on them that it was not going to be as easy buying a dog as they'd thought. I had to leave the room to ring their local council to check something they had told me, and when I returned, the son-in-law steamed into me. He accused me of being rude and ignorant and said that I needed to go back to school to learn some manners. He warned me that he was going to write to the Director General to complain about me.

'His mother-in-law grabbed my hand and said: "Don't worry, dear, it's all right. I think you're wonderful." Then she turned to her son-in-law and told him to stop shouting at me.

'It was a pretty ugly scene, which I'm sure wouldn't have happened had I not gone out of the room. In the time I was away, the tension they'd been feeling caused the man and his wife to have a row and he was fired up, ready to shoot me down. If I hadn't gone out, they would all have stormed off unhappily, but it would not have developed into what it did.

'After the man had finished bellowing at me I just said, very calmly: "Fair enough," and opened the door for them all to leave. I never argue with anyone; there's no point; you just go round in circles and could be there for ever. If someone can do what we ask and stick to what we feel is best for them, then, by all means, they can have a dog that is suitable. It's as simple as that.

'With this family, it was only the first interview. Goodness knows what their reaction would have been if they'd gone round and picked a dog and then been told they could not have it, because it was unsuitable. Looking back, I don't think I would have allowed a man like that to have a dog in any circumstances. Anyone who flipped like he did was unlikely to be a good owner.

'When I was interviewed to be a re-homer, we talked about dealing with someone who really pushed it and got very nasty. I was asked if I'd give in and let them have a dog – and I said: "No way. I'm not scared of anybody. I'd never let them wangle me into a corner and force me to do something I felt was wrong."

'A couple of days after I started re-homing, three huge brothers came in wanting a German Shepherd. They didn't give much away and I guessed they had something to hide. Eventually, they owned up that they had a dog, but could not bring it in to Battersea to meet the one they wanted to buy because it was chained up in their father's garage and they couldn't get near it. I was not convinced that they were not going to use the Shepherd as a guard dog, so I refused to let them have it. They were so gobsmacked that little me could stand there and say: "No. You're not having a dog," that they didn't argue. I just opened the door and they walked out. They were the first people I'd had to refuse and I was relieved they took it so well.'

Re-homers often have to be assertive with prospective buyers, but sometimes they take a subtle approach, giving reasons that may not be strictly justifiable, but ones they know the customer will accept.

Paul Wilkins remembers a very old man who insisted he wanted a puppy. Paul suggested a more mature dog, about six or seven years old, would be a better bet, but the man was set on a puppy. 'I couldn't tell him he shouldn't have a dog who was going to be around long after he had gone, so I talked about all the house-training and chewing of furniture,' Paul said. 'That did the trick. He went for an older dog and they got on really well.'

Panic buttons were installed in the walls of the interviewing rooms after a re-homer was attacked by an agitated customer, who leapt across the desk. But Paul was once so terrified by two burly, heavily-tattooed Cockneys, wearing earrings, that he did not press the button, in case it made matters worse.

He said: 'I upset them by insisting we made a home visit and one of them pushed a stick in front of my face and told me he was going to wrap it round my head. I told him, "Look, calm down – I'll get the supervisor. She'll be able to sort something out.".

'The men were drunk and I was certain that whoever came down would not let them take an animal away. But I had to say something to get out of the room. Once I was out, I summoned other staff, then called the police, who ordered the men off the premises. The whole experience scared me, because I honestly felt it wouldn't have taken much more for the men to have beaten me up. Sometimes you can defuse tense situations by playing along with the customer, but these two were rough types from Peckham who were hardly likely to be placated that way.'

Another encounter with a drunk had a much happier outcome for Paul, however. She was a woman who said her name was Lola, and she turned up at Battersea's rear entrance after closing time, sobbing over her lost dog. She was in such a state that Paul made an exception and let her look round the kennels. Once inside, she became very aggressive and abusive, and male members of staff and some of the braver women hid round corners, ready to go to Paul's aid if she turned violent, too. They were not needed, because the minute Paul chatted to her about the famous Kinks' song that bore her name, the woman took his arm and started dancing along the line of kennels with him. They did not find the lost dog but, when they reached the gate, the woman thanked Paul for letting her in, and asked if he minded her kissing him.

'I was shocked and embarrassed, but I didn't like to be rude,' said Paul. 'So,

This is one of the many happy re-homings. Sadly for the staff, occasionally members of the public can be very difficult, at times even violent, and interviews can end on a sour note.

I let her give me a big smacker on the lips. I've never had a kiss like that before. The woman had no teeth!'

Sometimes drunks do get violent. May Whammond remembers one woman who could not find her lost mongrel in Tealby and took it out on her.

'She grabbed me by the jumper and pinned me against the wall,' said May. 'I warned her not to intimidate me and fortunately she saw sense. But the aggravation didn't end there. The woman assumed that every lost dog ended up in Battersea and wouldn't accept that hers wasn't here. She even accused me of hiding it and I had to insist that she went along all the aisles looking in every kennel to put her mind at rest.'

Michelle Ritter has never been threatened, but she was called all sorts of names by a man she refused to sell a Border Collie.

She said: 'The dog was neurotic and had behaviour problems. We were

114

looking for someone who had a Collie with similar problems and this man hadn't. He could not understand what I was talking about and stormed off, calling me names. I thought: "With a temper like that, how are you going to cope with a dog that misbehaves?"'

If a member of the public cannot understand why one of the staff will not sell them a dog, or will not release a stray or badly-treated rescue dog from Tealby, they usually demand to see a supervisor – either Mel Wareham or Jackie Donaghy. They are Battersea's troubleshooters. And the 'front line' action they have to face is often frighteningly dangerous.

Jackie said: 'It's almost "Put the body armour on and go down!" I'm the one who deals with people coming to claim their Pit Bulls. Usually, I can deal with it: I have to explain that their dog is very nice, but we are governed by law and can't release it. I will say: "We'll try to help you, though." It is not lying. If you hit aggro with aggro, you get it. We have to protect ourselves, save our own lives!

'Recently I got a phone call from Battersea police, warning me that a bloke whose Pit Bull we were holding had a record of all sorts of serious offences, including grievous bodily harm and arson. They assured me he wouldn't come to the Home, because he knew his dog was illegal. But he did.

'He was a Cockney, with tattoos and scars and broken teeth. And he said he wanted his dog back and he wasn't going to pay anything for it and, if he didn't get it, he was going to burn the place down.

'I was really scared of him and felt like crying. I rang the police and three of them arrived, one in a bullet-proof jacket. They convinced the Cockney he couldn't have his dog and he asked if he could buy another one. I told him we would get in touch with him – anything to get him off the premises. When he had gone, I couldn't believe how much I was shaking.

'We were all so worried that, for the next few days, we had the police on stand-by, in case he carried out his threat to torch the Home. That sort of person thinks they're beyond the law. He was trying to con us that his dog was registered, but we knew it was not.

'Mel and I have had to deal with dozens of explosive people down the years, and I've often said to our manager, Nichola, that I don't get paid enough for worrying about whether I'm going to be punched or stabbed – or whatever! We either need classes in self-defence or a screen to hide behind when we tell people they can't have what they want.

'A bloke did try to stab me once. His dog – a gorgeous Whippet puppy – had been brought in as a stray and I was refusing to let him take it back, because he had been seen beating it up.

'He came in with a young girl, who turned out to be his girlfriend, and a little boy, who was wearing no shoes. The guy was out of control and suddenly, in the middle of the heated conversation, he pulled out a knife and lunged at me.

I ran, terrified, up to Nichola's office, but she wasn't there. I didn't know what to do for the best. Gradually, my terror turned to anger. I thought: "Why do I have to put up with this?" A few minutes later, I went back and confronted him. I was seething. I glared at him and said loudly: "Right. You sit straight down. Now! And you do NOT threaten me any more. I will not take it. You do NOT get your dog back yet." Inwardly, I was praying.

'Going on the attack did the trick. "What do you want me to do?" he said, meekly. "Put my hands on my head like a child?"

'"You can do whatever you like," I said. "But you'll sit there till I've spoken to the dog warden."

'Then I stormed upstairs to my office and collapsed in a chair, heart pumping.

'I learned that the RSPCA had been to the man's house with a policeman after neighbours had rung about the dog being repeatedly ill-treated. The owner punched the policeman in the face and shut the door. He had been arrested and charged with assault, then Social Services got involved, because the man's very young girlfriend and their baby boy had been beaten as well. The guy was desperate to get his dog back, but had to accept that it was an RSPCA cruelty case and we were entitled to keep it.

'When the situation was finalized and they left, I got a call from Social Services, asking if I'd seen any bruises on the child. "I'm sorry," I said. "I didn't notice. I felt my life was at stake at the time."'

The rule forbidding strays from being sold for seven days is often infuriating. It means, sometimes, that nothing can stop an owner re-claiming a dog, that Battersea suspect they have ill-treated. Once they have left Battersea, there is nothing the staff can do. Jackie has found a way to keep an eye on dubious owners: she has cultivated friendships with four RSPCA inspectors who are more than happy to visit homes where Jackie suspects a dog is in danger.

Another time Jackie was really frightened was when she was re-homing a few years ago.

'This weird skinhead with huge, piercing blue eyes, came for a dog with his wife,' she said. 'It seemed he had something to prove, because he found fault with every dog we suggested was suitable. Eventually he lost his rag and his wife told him off. He turned round and whacked her round the face, then stormed out.

'The wife told me he was a right pig at home; she could never do anything right. If she left him, he would make her life worse.

'I said: "I'm not being funny, but I would not dream of putting a dog in your situation."

'She said she had better go after him, or he would make her life a misery. I was just thinking myself lucky I'd never have to speak to him again when he burst in, held a fist against my chin, and started shouting and swearing at me. I can't remember all he said, but the gist of it was that we, at Battersea, thought we knew it all.

'I just held my breath, thinking: "This is all going to be over in a minute; he's either going to hurt me or walk off." Fortunately, it was the latter. He suddenly went quiet, then stormed out, slamming doors.

'The shock of it all took a few seconds to hit me. Then I screamed. I'd rather deal with Pit Bulls than a lot of the thugs we get here. Some dogs have got a bad name, but it is people who are the problem.'

Jackie was particularly taken with a pretty Border Collie found wandering in Wandsworth. And when she discovered it was suffering from dwarfism and unlikely to live more than another two and a half years, she knew she had to find a perfect home. Sadly, she found herself in a distressing sequence of events that upset her so much it made her think that Battersea was, perhaps, failing in its job.

She said: 'The poor little thing was going to be forever puppy-sized, which endeared it to me even more. One of our home visitors, who deals with Collies and working dogs, knew someone who would make an ideal owner. But before the dog had completed its seven days on the stray block, a big bloke, in a filthy T-shirt and equally dirty, baggy jeans, came in, saying the dog was his and he wanted it back. He was an odd-looking bloke, who looked as though he had not washed for days, and sounded a bit simple. He had his mother with him – a bearded lady wearing trousers under a dress, who reeked of urine.

'The Collie had come in with two other dogs – a fat Labrador-cross with overgrown nails and warts, aged about 16; and a long-haired mongrel about the same age. The dog warden told me the woman had signed the dogs over to him because she no longer wanted them. And I was not to give them back.

'The woman, however, told me she had given the dogs away because she was stressed at being threatened with eviction from her home on the Peabody Estate, which did not allow dogs. She planned to take the older dogs to a vet, who would re-home them, and sell the Collie to one of her son's friends in Peckham.

'"Leave the little one with us," I said. "We can find a perfect home."

'The woman's oddball son intervened: "I ain't leaving here without that dog," he said, aggressively. "Listen, I'm a security guard. I'm phoning my solicitor." With that, he started tapping out numbers on a mobile phone, then pretended to speak to someone. It was obvious that the phone was not working. Then he demanded to see the manager.

'I knew that if Nichola came down, by law, she would have to allow them to have the dog, so I told them she was at lunch. He said they would wait.

'I begged and pleaded with them for three hours, but they still wanted to see the manager. I went upstairs, red in the face and tearful from all the tension and told Nichola the whole story. "Please back me on this," I said. "They're not equipped to keep any dog, let alone one that is going to have enormous problems."

'Nichola calmed me and we both went downstairs. "Right," she said to the weirdo. "It's your dog. What are you going to do with it?"

'Arrogantly, he replied: "I might give it to my mate. I might give it back to my Mum. I might keep it."

'Nichola said: "If we give you your dog back, we're going to send someone round to make sure it's being cared for."

'"No problem," the bloke said.

'Nichola turned to me. "Jackie, will you give this gentleman his dog back."

'Dreadfully upset, I went upstairs and opened the Collie's kennel: he jumped up and started licking my face furiously. I fell on the floor cuddling him and bawling my eyes out. One of the girls came in, shocked, and asked me what was the matter, but I was so wrecked I couldn't speak.

'I knew there was no way I could talk to the idiot again because I'd be in danger of losing my job – big time. So I just cuddled and stroked the Collie and said, "You poor little thing," then handed him to May Whammond to take downstairs. I stood at the window, sobbing, as I watched mother and son take the dog. The poor little thing had been with us only a day, but my heart went out with him.

'I went to the office, where Mel made coffee and gave me a cigarette, and finally made me stop wailing. But I was still desperately worried about the little mite. One of the staff, who lived in Wandsworth, near the Peabody Estate, said she would put my mind at rest by popping round to the woman's flat that night. She went on the pretext of giving her some dog food, but discovered the dog had gone; presumably to the son's friend in Peckham. While she was there, she saw there was no furniture in the flat, except a settee, which both mother and son slept on!

'We never saw that dear little Collie again. I knew we wouldn't. I was so angry with the whole system, it made me think: If we can't win a battle for a dog like that, what's the point of working here?'

Battersea's other trouble-shooter, Mel Wareham, said: 'I'll never forget the woman who came in wanting a dog and told me, rather proudly, that she had owned five dogs – two Staffordshire Bull Terriers, a Rottweiler, a German Shepherd and a Pit Bull. The Staffs had been run over; she had given the Rottie away; the Shepherd had run off; the Pit Bull had been shot by the police.

'There was absolutely no way – whatever her circumstances then – that I was going to allow her to buy a dog. There was no point arranging a home visit because she could live in a palace and she still wouldn't be suitable for a

Battersea dog. In the nicest possible way I had to be blunt: "I'm terribly sorry. Thank you so much for coming here and filling in a form, but we cannot continue with your application on the strength of your dog-keeping history."

'The woman argued the toss but she had no chance of changing my mind. Sometimes people keep on and on, and we have to cut things off and almost walk out the door. Otherwise it's like a tennis match. But we are always professional and polite and never lose our temper. I've been close to it, however!

'The situations where I don't have to control my temper, but do get very disillusioned, are when a family with young children try to persuade us to sell them a dog we have specifically marked: "Not suitable for children." This is quite obviously not Battersea being child-unfriendly or deliberately perverse – it is simply that the dog may be food or toy possessive, or have some behaviour trait that could endanger a child. But, often, parents will argue with us, saying: "Can't we just give it a go?" I'll say: "What happens if the dog bites your child? You have given it a go – and now your child is maimed for life and terrified of dogs. And the animal has to be put to sleep." It's truly terrifying how many people would actually put their own children in danger.'

While much of the upset and irritation suffered by Battersea's staff is fuelled by the emotional state of the people they deal with, their patience is also tried by people arriving without checking the procedure they are expected to go through. Even today, people turn up thinking they can make a token donation and walk away with a dog. Countless others arrive without the necessary documents required to prove who they are and where they live. This is infuriating for staff: it not only wastes time they could be spending on customers who *have* come prepared, but it adds to the tension of an emotionally-charged experience.

What does not help either, are the mindless young people who think it amusing to breeze into Battersea after a couple too many in the pub and pretend to be interested in buying a dog. They waste the staff's time and Ann Challis, the Home Visitor's, too: she has lost count of the number of wild-goose chases she has been on, to roads where the numbers run out, or to addresses that do not exist.

She said: 'The minute I say I'm from the Dogs' Home and a mother, say, greets me with a laugh, I know I'm on a fool's errand. Her teenage son probably had a Sunday lunchtime drink and thought it a good idea to go to Battersea with his mates and get himself a Rottweiler.

'Obviously it's a waste of time we can all do without, but there's nothing we can do about it. The re-homer's card would probably mention something about the bloke having had a drink, but we still have to check it out.

'What annoys me is turning up somewhere, having made an appointment, to find no one in. People do that because they don't want you to see how they live.

That's why I don't make many appointments. I find it best to turn up unexpectedly and find people as they really are.'

One such impromptu visit ended with Ann feeling she was lucky to get away with a verbal assault, not a bashing. Battersea had asked her to see a couple – living with their four children, under six, in a small flat – who were keen to buy a male Doberman.

'The husband, very rough and ready and several years older than his wife, could not see why the choice of dog was wrong,' said Ann. 'After giving me a lot of verbal abuse, he told me he didn't have to take a stray from Battersea – he could simply go out and spend £1000 on any dog he liked. I suggested, as courteously as I could, that if that was how he felt, that's precisely what he should do, because I was most certainly not going to put a Doberman into their situation.

'I didn't go on the attack. I didn't say: "You can't have a dog." I wanted to talk about the sort of dog that would fit into their lifestyle, given the lack of space and children etc. But the guy was full of himself and didn't like being told what he didn't want to hear. I feel I was lucky he was only rude because I honestly felt he was going to wallop me.'

Despite Battersea's efforts to broker perfect 'marriages', nobody can guarantee that circumstances will not change. As streamlined as the procedure is, Ann had a very sad experience, where a Battersea dog's life had changed for the worse. One day, a man phoned about a German Shepherd, owned by a neighbour, who was an alcoholic and going through a painful divorce. The dog was not being cared for, and the neighbour was worried for it because the owner also had epilepsy.

When Ann made a surprise visit to the owner's house, in Ilford, Essex, it looked as though no one was living there: the curtains were drawn, there was junk mail in the letterbox, free newspapers on the doorstep, and when Ann knocked, no one answered. At the back, there was dog's mess everywhere – chalky white, indicating that the dog was eating a lot of bones. Confused, Ann went home to Dartford, in Kent, and, that evening, phoned the house. A man answered. When she said she wanted to visit to see how his dog was, he agreed immediately: he was polite, helpful and sounded very together.

When Ann turned up the next day, however, no one seemed in. The only change was that there was more dog's mess at the back and rubbish bags had been emptied all over the garden. Ann was wondering what to do for the best when the man opened the back door. He smelled strongly of drink.

Ann spoke to him briefly, then asked where his dog was. The man said he was upstairs and agreed for her to go up. Ann went into a spare bedroom and found a beautiful black and gold Shepherd lying on his side in the middle of the room. He made no sound as Ann went up to him, nor made the slightest movement with his tail. He just lay there, looking at her with mournful eyes. Ann asked the dog's name – Shadow – and made a fuss of him. Eventually, he got up and Ann was concerned to see how thin he was. She asked if Shadow was eating anything. The man took her downstairs into the kitchen. He opened the freezer: it was packed with dog food.

Ann said there must be something seriously wrong for Shadow to lose so much weight, if he was eating normally. She told the man to book an appointment with his vet and she would come back in a week. When she went back, however, no one answered either the front or back doors, and the garden was in an even worse state.

'Fearing something terrible had happened, I phoned the police and two burly police constables turned up,' said Ann. 'One of them was just forcing open the patio windows when the man drove up – with Shadow – wondering what was going on. He was a little drunk, but the police ignored it: they were relieved he was safe – and embarrassed that they were forcing their way into his home.

'The man said he had been to the vet, but Shadow was still losing weight. I advised Battersea that the dog should be taken from the house, but we have no authority to take dogs away from their owners. I was so worried, I drove to the house two days later to see what was happening. The man was drunk. I got the feeling he was always too drunk to get the dog's food out of the freezer, because rubbish bags had been ripped open again, and it was obvious Shadow had been looking for food.

'I said it was best if I took the dog to Battersea, but the man didn't want that; Shadow was his best mate, he said. I dug my heels in: either I took him with me there and then, I said, or I'd contact the RSPCA who would definitely remove him. Reluctantly, the man agreed and I took Shadow to Battersea. It was terribly sad, watching the man say goodbye to his friend, but I knew it would be better for both of them in the long run.

'I was very worried about the man, too. He obviously wasn't eating regularly either and was thinner every time I saw him. I contacted the police and told them my fears, but they could not help. Now the dog was not there, they were powerless to do anything.'

It was a sad experience but, happily, Shadow was re-homed, and his new owners soon brought some much-needed sunshine into his life.

OVERLEAF: Head of Re-homing, Mel Wareham saying goodbye to one of her favourite residents in the courtyard outside Kent Kennels.

CHAPTER EIGHT

Farewell, my lovely – we'll all miss you

For the staff, saying goodbye to a dog walking out on to Battersea Park Road with a new owner is a bitter-sweet experience. They appreciate they have been just a temporary refuge; a stopping-off point before the animal moves to somewhere more comfortable, where the memories of all those lonely hours behind bars can be erased and replaced with love and affection from someone more permanent.

They understand that finding homes is what Battersea is all about; that all those nips and tucks, the tireless grooming, the socializing and fostering and the work in Rehab – have all been geared to this poignant parting at the exit door. But that does not mean that saying farewell to a dog they have helped transform and come to adore is not a huge emotional wrench.

It does not mean the young men and women of Battersea don't weep buckets, watching the animals walk out of their lives. For when a dog comes into your life, there is a deal, and the deal is that it gives you its heart, but when it leaves, it takes a piece of yours.

After the tears have dried and they have consoled themselves with positive thoughts about the dog's future, the staff get on with the job. But the memories of their favourites – particularly those adorable old dogs who did not sell themselves well, who stayed rather too long – never leave them, and, often, they find themselves wondering about them. Sometimes, there will be a nagging worry: has the once-destructive Lurcher returned to his old ways? What about that poor Greyhound's anxiety attacks? Has that Shepherd started biting dogs again?

None of the staff expects regular progress reports, but they are delighted when photographs arrive, showing a dog they remember being depressed, now bounding along in a park or frolicking in the sea; or one that was always rocketing round its kennel in frustration, now reclining, in regal splendour, on velvet sofa cushions. The photos will be passed round, excitedly, and then given pride of place on the staff notice board.

Michelle Ritter remembers how thrilled everyone was to receive 24 pictures of Buster, a two-year-old Shepherd-cross, who had been at Battersea a year: he was so

erratic in his kennel they were beginning to fear that no one would ever want him.

Buster, the Shepherd-cross, who was not the best advert for himself.

'Buster was not the best advert for himself,' said Michelle. 'People looking for a pet don't want one that is doing the Wall of Death round his cage. In the end, we put him on *Pet Rescue* and were inundated with offers. Buster could not cope with kennel life, but once outside, he was a different dog. Even we were suprised at how calm and well behaved he was during filming. He went to a wonderful couple in Windsor, who sent me photographs of Buster in different situations, all neatly labelled: "Buster in the car ... Buster in the garden ... Buster in the park ... Buster in the front room" etc. It was wonderful of them to think of us. Buster had come in badly beaten and they obviously knew how much work we had put into him.'

Michelle Ritter, the proud foster mum, who never lost faith that Urcher would find a loving home.

One ecstatic owner even sent an hour-long video starring another Shepherd-cross, called Juliette, which had been so ill and depressed she was always in and out of the pharmacy. The staff prayed she would catch someone's eye in the 1997 pre-Christmas rush, but she was still there afterwards and sadly, started going really downhill.

'We were desperately upset and worried and thought she would never go,' said Ann O'Brien. 'But, then, a couple from the north of England, who had had to have their dog put to sleep three months before, were in London for the day and decided to pop in on the off-chance. They fell in love with Juliette and she took to them. Two weeks later, we were sent a video, showing Juliette having her first bath, her first trip to the beach, her first this and that. It was like a video parents would take of their baby. We were thrilled to bits for Juliette, of course, but we were touched by the couple's gesture for ourselves, too. Not everyone appreciates the hard work and love that Battersea puts into the dogs.'

For Ann and her colleagues, the Juliettes are the highs of their Battersea lives. Having seen a dog arrive, confused and stressed, and comforted it at its lowest ebb, then trained all the fear and aggression and nervousness out of it, to the point when someone comes along and says, 'That looks a lovely dog – that's the one I want,' is what makes them go to work in the morning. But there is another kind of high – a more profound, intense one – that, when it comes, is an exhilarating experience that fills everyone at Battersea with the warmest inner glow and makes their jobs even more deeply satisfying and rewarding. For Michelle, such an experience came after she committed herself to transforming a lovable Lurcher that had been on the sales block for 18 months. Both of them suffered an agonizing, bumpy roller-coaster ride of emotion before Michelle achieved what she had begun to think was impossible.

Someone had amusingly named the Lurcher, Urcher, and he had become Battersea's most famous 'long-stayer' – the name staff give to those dogs who, for one reason or another, do not appeal to prospective buyers and stay on the sales block longer than usual, sometimes for years.

Urcher was brought in covered in fleas and mange, and weighing half what he should have, in February 1995, after being found by police on a gipsy site. He had no behavioural problems and was loved by the staff, who considered him a bit of a character. But he was one of the unlucky dogs few would-be buyers showed interest in and the less human contact he had, the more he withdrew into himself. Sadly, as the months wore on, he developed dog-to-dog aggression, which made it extremely difficult to find people willing to take him on. Even if someone was prepared to take a chance, Jackie Donaghy and her team felt that it would not work out, and Urcher would soon be back.

After Urcher had been in Battersea for fourteen months, Jackie decided something had to be done: the poor, unhappy boy was in a dark tunnel and there seemed not the merest hint of any light at the end of it. Michelle Ritter did not have any pets, so Jackie asked her to foster Urcher. Michelle worked hard at restoring Urcher's confidence in human contact and got him used to being cuddled. Within three months, he had become affectionate to her, but the dog aggression remained a problem – a big one.

When Michelle took him to Battersea Park the first thought on Urcher's mind, it seemed, was sorting out another dog: even if one was 100 yards away, Urcher would be up on his hind legs, roaring at it and straining at the leash. No doubt he would have steamed in, no holds barred and caused serious damage, if Michelle had not held on – tight.

It took Michelle six months to calm Urcher down at the sight of another dog. Then, she tried him off the lead with other Battersea dogs on the new land; if he was going to bite a dog, she reasoned, it was best it was one of their own, not one belonging to a member of the public. Urcher mixed well with the other dogs, but he was rather bad mannered, with little social etiquette:

Urcher, the Lurcher, Battersea's longest stayer before his appearance on TV led to 350 inquiries – and a marvellous new home.

A HEALTHY DOG

A healthy dog has a good
appetite, but watch out for
excessive thirst.

A wet nose is not important,
but there should be no
discharge from the nose.

The coat should be lustrous,
without baldness, excessive
greasiness or itchiness.

Ears should be clean and free
of odour. Look out for
excessive head shaking.

Eyes should be bright and
there should be no evidence
of discharge.

The dog's motions should
be normal.

Teeth should be free of plaque
and the gums pink.

When exercising, there should
be no shortness of breath.

while other dogs approached each other gently and had a sniff around before starting to play, Urcher would barge in, often knocking a dog to the ground, then run off, as if to say: 'Come on, chase me, then.'

'At that time, he had no idea of the rules of playing,' said Michelle. 'He was very much in your face – "Bosh, you will play with me!" But the other dog would back off, terrified.'

Fortunately, Michelle lived near Southwark Park, in Rother-hithe, south-east London, and she walked Urcher there every evening. She kept him muzzled, and on the lead, but he did seem calmer with all the different dogs he got to know. Michelle was thrilled: all her patience and hard work seemed to be paying off. She felt she was winning. She even dared hope that Urcher might be well enough to be put up for re-homing again in the New Year. And then, one evening, a few days before Christmas 1996, approaching the end of Urcher's second year as a Battersea dog, something happened that dashed all her hopes and ruined all the progress Urcher had made.

Michelle was returning to her flat after work, with Urcher on his lead. Suddenly – out of nowhere, it seemed – a vicious Staffordshire Bull Terrier flew at Urcher from behind, attacking his back legs again and again. Michelle kept trying to pull the Staff off, but he was a fighting dog and too strong.

'I knew it was a fighter, because it made no sound while attacking,' Michelle said. 'It just charged up and kept attacking. It would have gone for any dog on sight.

'I didn't know what to do for the best. At first, I held the lead tight to stop Urcher fighting back. But, in the end, I was so worried he was getting hurt, I had to give him his head so that he could defend himself. But he didn't; he was too scared, because he could not match the other dog's aggression. He tried to submit, but, being a fighting dog, the Staff ignored – or didn't understand – Urcher's body language. If it hadn't been a fighter, and Urcher had submitted, it would have walked off, thinking: "Hah. Won that one."

'The owner was watching from a nearby flat and I kept shouting at him to do something, but he didn't seem interested. He was one of those know-it-all south London lads in his twenties who owned a status Staff! He could not care less. Finally, things got so bad, he did come and get his dog off Urcher, but the damage had been done. There was no muscle tear – just surface wounds – but Urcher was so traumatized, I could not continue socializing him. I had to walk him on the new land at the rear of the Home on his own.'

Urcher celebrated his second year in Battersea in February 1997 and, as she had done the previous year, Michelle decorated his kennel with coloured streamers and mobiles. And she put a card on the door, with a moving poem about him: a positive statement that it was a birthday anniversary not a negative one, marking another year in captivity.

Would-be buyers were drawn to the colourful kennel and several showed a fleeting interest in Urcher, but no one wanted him. One of the reasons was his attitude when visitors looked at him: Unlike most other dogs in Battersea and Bell Mead, he did not jump up and start performing the moment the public arrived. He made no effort to sell himself; he just lay there, as if to say: "I don't know why you're looking at me – I don't need a home – I have Michelle, she's my Mum."

The bond between them had, indeed, deepened: Urcher was increasingly affectionate to Michelle and behaving even better with four Dalmatians and a black mongrel he met every evening in Southwark Park; he was now confident enough to go up and greet them. The other owners had taken a liking to Urcher and always asked how he was coming along. One evening one of them suggested Michelle let him off the lead to see what happened. Michelle was a little dubious, but agreed; she, too, wanted to see how Urcher behaved.

'We were walking in an enclosure, about the size of a football pitch, so I didn't have the worry of Urcher running off and hurting other people's dogs. But it was the first time I'd let him off the lead and I was very nervous. He was a bit rough in play and the other dogs kept their distance; it was as though they realized he was a grumpy old man. But, generally, they all liked each other and ran around together, playing happily. Those images of him on his hind legs, roaring at dogs in the other side of the park, were still strong in my mind and to see him running around with five dogs was stunning. I was a very proud Mum that evening. More important, it gave me confidence that he was now suitable for re-homing.'

Unfortunately, Urcher was still not interested in selling himself to prospective buyers and, throughout the spring and summer, there were only three serious inquiries about him. They all came to nothing. Despite her bright, breezy nature and positive attitude, Michelle became despondent. And just when she thought that things could not get any worse, they did. It was August and Michelle was walking Urcher in Battersea Park; he was off his lead, but muzzled. He had grown in confidence and bounded over to a German Shepherd, fifty yards or so away, and barged into him. Minutes later, he limped back to Michelle, and she was distressed to see an eight-inch tear in his thigh.

'It was a horrible open wound and I could see all the muscles inside,' Michelle said. 'The owner claimed that Urcher had run into a stick, but I didn't believe him; Urcher had teeth marks on the inside of his thigh. How he got the injury didn't matter, though. The bottom line was that he'd had another major

Bruce (left) and Beano.
Two unwanted dogs who
found boundless love –
not to mention a cosy
velvet rug amid ten
country acres.

130

setback and faced more time out from being socialized. We were all terribly upset and wondered just what the future held for him.'

What it held came in the form of a phone call from *Pet Rescue*, a month later. Did Battersea have a dog they felt particularly suitable for an appeal? Urcher was the obvious choice. And after he appeared, Battersea got a staggering 350 inquiries from people throughout the country eager to give him a home. One couple – Joe and Jane Belasco – sounded particularly ideal: over the years they had had St Bernards, Labradors and various mongrels and, vitally important, had rescued a Lurcher bitch which had experienced similar problems to Urcher.

Michelle said: 'It was stunningly obvious that the couple could offer Urcher the most marvellous home, but Bella, their Lurcher, was very much their baby and if Urcher was the least bit grouchy with her, the couple said they could not entertain having him. The dogs met and seemed to like each other. But we still had a problem: Bella considered the family car hers. Would she let Urcher into it? She was as good as gold. She jumped on the front passenger seat, next to Joe, where she always sat, and Urcher went in the back with Jane.'

Watching them drive off to the family home, near Colchester, Michelle wept buckets. Urcher did not give a backward glance. Early in December 1997, the Belascos invited Michelle to their home to see how Urcher was getting on. She accepted, but was concerned she might unsettle him. She need not have worried: Urcher gave her five minutes' attention, then went off to play with Bella in the garden.

Michelle was relieved. She said: 'It was as if he was saying: "This is my home now. I remember you – and you were nice. But I prefer it here." And who can blame him?'

Few people liked Bruce and Beano. They were huge dogs who had been in Battersea more than a year and, it seemed, were destined never to be re-homed. Bruce was a Shepherd-Lurcher cross, about six, and he bit people who put their hands through the bars of his kennel. He did not get out much until Jade Hall started working on his block. She loves older dogs and saw something in Bruce that others did not – something special. She started taking him for walks in Battersea Park.

Beano was a tan Doberman-Lurcher cross, about eight, and nobody wanted him, either. He was not suited to living in a built-up area and did not seem to have much longer to live. But Jade fell in love with him, too. She saw a gangly, gentle giant with a heart of gold, who would not hurt a fly.

The dogs were opposites: Beano loved his food and other dogs; Bruce loved his squeaky toys more than anything else in the world and was indifferent to all other dogs. But they never squabbled; they just revelled in being out with Jade, tugging her along excitedly on their leads, and ignored each other. Jade took those two huge, different dogs out every day for almost a year. But they always came back to their kennels and stayed there. They were still the dogs nobody wanted.

When it was decided to send Beano to Bell Mead to give him another chance, Jade was heartbroken: she had become so close to him and did not want to let him go. But she knew it was best. She consoled herself that the 'breath of fresh country air' that Bell Mead offered would do him the world of good; and, who knows, she thought, someone might come along and see in him what she did, and make him happy for what little time he had left.

A month later, Jade went to Bell Mead to visit Beano. She came away more upset than she had been in her life. The dog just sat, sad and lonely and confused, in his kennel. He did not seem to have any friends. And he did not have Jade, who knew how to get the best out of him. He was worse off than he had been at Battersea. Driving away from Bell Mead, Jade knew what she had to do: she had to try to find him a home herself. Before it was too late.

And then Bruce bit another visitor, who put her hand through the bars of his kennel, and he, too, was moved to Bell Mead. Jade was distraught, fearing both dogs would go downhill fast and die there. She went home to Wiltshire and persuaded pet shops, libraries, vets and general retailers in Salisbury to put up posters, appealing for homes for Beano and Bruce, but the months went by and no one wanted to know. Jade began to despair.

And then she was transferred from Battersea's kennels to join the re-homing team – and, within a few weeks, the lives of her unwanted boys miraculously changed.

Jade said: 'I pressed the ticket machine and called out, "Number 71". A little lady with white hair said: "That's me," and we went into an interview room. I liked her on sight.

'"Right, dear," she said. "All I want is a dog nobody else wants."

'I couldn't believe what I was hearing. "Don't move," I said, and left the room to get both my boys' assessments. I came back, eager to show them to the lady but she was not interested in looking at them.

'"I have got two dogs," I told her. "Bruce and Beano. Beano's old and big and gorgeous with a heart of gold. And there's Bruce. He's a biter, but lovely, too."

'She said: "The biting doesn't bother me – I've lived with that before. I'll take both of them." I almost wanted to drag her to my locker where I had photos of them, but she did not want to know anything about them. That they were unwanted and in need of a good home was all that concerned her.

'She told me she lived in Durham and was in London visiting her daughter, Denise, who was a barrister. She said that she had had lots of dogs, some with problems, and the last one had only recently died. There were not many strays in Durham, so she wanted to rescue one from London. She lived in the country, with her husband and brother, in ten acres of land.

'Everything was right. I couldn't believe it. I thought: "You're perfect." To be honest, she was so genuine, so nice, I would have given her anything. But I had to check her out for my boys' sake. I took her name – Beatrice, it was – and rang her vet in Durham who knew her well.

'"Beatrice!" said the vet. "How fantastic. Give her anything. They have got ten acres. The family love their animals more than anything in the world. I recommend them 100 per cent."

'I thought: "How wonderful." I then rang and spoke to Beatrice's husband and brother, who sounded as lovely as her. Next, I asked my supervisor, Mel Wareham, if we could break with our usual policy of not re-homing two big male dogs together. Fortunately, Mel trusted my judgement and gave the go-ahead for Beatrice and Denise to pick up Beano and Bruce the following day.

'They picked the dogs up the moment Bell Mead opened the next morning. Denise had an important meeting she couldn't cancel, so the dogs spent the day in her chambers, lazing around on sofa cushions and being fussed over by everyone who came in. Bruce seemed particularly at home, tail wagging furiously as he showed visitors his "Kong" toy. A secretary fed them chocolate biscuits and they generally took it easy until the evening when Denise drove them all to Durham in her Range Rover. Bruce, apparently, spread out on the back seat, while Beano was on two woolly rugs in the rear compartment. They were no trouble at all on the 300-mile journey.

'After meeting Beatrice's horse and mooching round the moonlit fields at 1.00 am, the dogs fell asleep in the kitchen, on a sofa, covered by a huge velvet rug, Beano's chin and ears cradled in Denise's arm, Bruce's head in her uncle's lap. They woke briefly when everyone went to bed, but then snuggled down together and were still sleeping when Beatrice and Denise came down at 7.00 am.

'By 7.03 am, however, they were both haring around the fields, excited by all the new smells and trails. Ten minutes later they were called for breakfast and came in immediately – albeit stinking from rolling around in fresh rabbit droppings! Over the next few days, they settled in and became such a well-loved part of the home, it was as though they had been living there all their lives.'

RIGHT: Bruce, the gangly giant with a heart of gold, who now has his own spacious paddock.

That was in October, 1997. In February this year, Jade was sent on a behavioural course near Durham and wrote to Beatrice, asking if she could pop by and say hello to the boys. Beatrice told her she was more than welcome, but needed to know that, very sadly, Beano had passed away. Jade *did* go to Durham – with Michelle Ritter – and had

134

a wonderful evening. Beano was not mentioned once; Beatrice and her family had come to love him so much they were not able to talk about him.

But Bruce, it was clear, had it made. The family's life revolves around him: because of his tendency to bite, all their friends phone before dropping in; he has dozens of squeaky toys, all carefully wrapped in socks because he tries to destroy them as quickly as possible. And he has his own spacious paddock, equipped with reflective strips, so that he can charge around at night and not hurt himself. Some might say he is spoilt rotten. Others – probably the majority – would say: 'After what he's been through, why not?'

Jarvis, a lovable, excitable and cheeky Saluki-cross, was four months old when he was found wandering along the M40, emaciated and riddled with fleas. He was put in Battersea's nursery, where he was bathed, fattened up and encouraged to socialize with other puppies and people. Sadly, when he was ready for re-homing, a plastic bed, filled with old newspapers, fell on him, fracturing his left back leg in several places. Over the next few months, the leg was cast many times, but was proving difficult to heal. Not surprisingly, poor Jarvis was frustrated and, whenever anyone passed his kennel, he would throw himself around crazily, for attention. He needed to be re-homed quickly or he was in danger of breaking more bones – so Jade Hall decided to foster him.

'He was like a wild animal when I took him,' she said. 'After spending so long cooped up in a kennel, he shot around my flat like a rocket – even though he couldn't use one of his legs and just dragged it behind. My own dog, Marley, did a good job of curbing his wild behaviour and, after a few days, Jarvis had burned off his pent-up energy and learned what to chew and what not.'

That back leg was useless, however, and Shaun Opperman decided it was best to amputate it. Jarvis did not mind in the least; he had not been using it for months anyway. What he did need now was a permanent home – one that could cope with an excitable, energetic youngster. Through a friend, Jade heard of a caring couple, who had a two-year-old female Afghan hound, called Darcy, who also used to bounce off walls when she was a puppy.

The couple sounded perfect, so Jade and her mum took Jarvis to their home. He had a good look round, chased Darcy for a while, then took a 'Nylabone' from her toy box and jumped on the sofa, where he proceeded to chew it nonchalantly. For him, at least, the decision was made: he was staying. And he did. The couple – and Darcy – liked him, too, and Jarvis moved in officially the next day.

Woody, a German Shepherd brought in off the streets of north London, was so unhappy, he did not make a sound for months; he just lay in his kennel, mournfully watching people pass by, in silence. Now, thanks to Sue Oak, Battersea's

Systems Administrator, Woody's depression has lifted and he has found his voice, living in Cornwall, with her parents. He loves chasing rabbits and mice, but his diet is somewhat odd: he prefers rainwater, picks his own blackberries ... and helps himself to tomatoes from the greenhouse. There are fields all around the house but, sadly, Woody has an allergy to grass, so he goes to the beach for exercise. He loves swimming, but, being a city dog, took some time before he stopped trying to bite the sea! Sue's father restores fire engines and when Woody is not at the beach, he likes nothing better than to ride in one. Sitting proudly in the front seat, he shows not the merest sign of the once-sad dog who suffered in silence for so long.

Another Shepherd, called Oliver Twist, was as noisy as Woody was quiet. He had been in sales for more than three months and had a bark so loud no visitor dared look at him. He would leap up at the bars of his kennel, forcing everyone to cringe in terror and hurry on by. Everyone, that is, except one man, who Jade felt, might be an appropriate owner. The man, who had had big Shepherds all his life, was not fazed by Oliver's ferocious facade and asked Jade to bring him to an interview room. He took a finger of chocolate from a pocket, put it in his mouth, then crouched down next to Oliver, inviting him to take it. To Jade's amazement, the 'frightening' dog took the chocolate as gently and delicately as a baby. Fifteen minutes later, after the paperwork was completed, Oliver trotted out of Kent Kennels on the way to a new and happy life. For Jade, it was a quick, easy sale. And one of the most satisfying.

As much as she adores Shepherds, Jade is a Lurcher lover and she could not bear for Brin to be put to sleep just because he was stiffening up with arthritis, made worse by inactivity in an enclosed space. The dog had been in kennels for six months and did not look like ever being re-homed. Shaun Opperman felt they were being unfair, keeping him alive when his quality of life was so poor and showed no sign of improving.

'Give me a couple of weeks,' Jade begged. 'I'll find him a home.'

Over the next few days, she rang every rescue centre she could find, but no one wanted the lonely Lurcher. With time running out, Jade designed a poster – with an appealing photograph of Brin in the middle – and implored pet shops near her home, to put it in their windows. It did the trick: a young couple were moved by Brin's plight and travelled from Salisbury to see him. Happily, he was everything they wanted and they took him home the same day. That dog was the first Jade re-homed and she became great friends with his new owners. She keeps in touch and when she goes home is always thrilled to see Brin revelling in his new, fun-filled life, those miserable six months in kennels long forgotten.

LEFT: Fluke, the Shepherd, whose anxiety problems vanished after just three weeks in his new home.

OPPOSITE: Jarvis, the excitable Saluki-cross, happy on just three legs.

BELOW: Woody, the Shepherd, in one of the fire engines restored by Sue Oak's father, Norman.

Friday the 13th, last March, proved lucky for Fluke, a seven-year-old Shepherd with anxiety problems. After 18 months at Bell Mead, he went on *Pet Rescue* and attracted 306 inquiries. Three weeks later he was in a new home, with a couple, their two children, and another dog, and showing no signs of the destructiveness and dog-to-dog aggression that forced his previous owner to get rid of him.

Ruth Yates, a re-homer at Bell Mead, said: 'We all knew Fluke had a lovely character, and we're thrilled to hear that it's coming out as he gains confidence in his new surroundings. The dogs get on, and Fluke has even got brave enough to be a little naughty: after being praised for offering his paw, he discovered the trick was useful for opening sealed dustbins!

'Fluke goes for three walks a day and when another dog passes, he sits down immediately, more concerned with listening for his new Daddy's next instruction than wanting a fight. Fluke has his own chair and gets on well with the children and their mother. But he has bonded incredibly with his new Daddy. It's a real love affair.'

Usually, stray dogs come round after their confusing, often traumatic, seven days in Tealby. But one little black and white Border Collie-cross, which Mel Wareham named Pepy, was too petrified to be put up for sale. Mel was sure he would find a home. But he needed a lot of work first.

She put in that work herself, socializing Pepy with other dogs in the park and with her colleagues in the Battersea canteen. The dog took up much of her day, but her perseverance paid off: Pepy improved dramatically over a couple of months and when he went into the sales block, he was snapped up within days. Unfortunately, Pepy did not want to leave Mel and when it dawned on him he was leaving the Home with strangers, he started crying for her.

'It was so sad,' Mel said. 'I kept telling him, "Don't be thick, Pepy – go. This is the start of your life." But he just wanted to stay with me. The new owners knew I'd done a lot of work with him and insisted I went to their home in Croydon to see Pepy once he had settled in. When they left the Home, I went off on my own and had a good cry, because I knew I was going to miss him desperately. But I also knew that, as well as we look after the dogs, Battersea isn't a proper home for them – it's just a means to what, hopefully, is a happy ending.'

Three weeks later, Pepy's owners phoned Mel to say he was getting on fine, and to invite her for Sunday lunch so that she could see for herself. Mel arrived at the couple's first-floor flat excited at the thought of seeing the dog she had missed so much. When the door opened, Pepy went for her and throughout lunch, sat a few feet away, growling at her. At the time, Mel was shaken and upset; she could not understand it. Having been on dog behaviour courses since, however, she understands what had happened.

'The couple had spoilt Pepy beyond belief,' she said. 'All the time he was with me, he knew his place and accepted I was in charge. They had elevated him to human status – even buying him his own three-piece suite! – and he had become impossibly dominant. He saw himself as the pack leader and didn't want anyone challenging his new position. The couple should have laid down ground rules early, but they didn't and, consequently, made a rod for their own backs. All the hard work I'd put in had gone out the window and Pepy was out of control.

'Now, our assessments would reveal if a dog had dominant tendencies and we wouldn't dream of re-homing one to fluffy-bunny owners.'

Veronique Cezerat is from southern France, and she fell in love with a gorgeous eight-year-old black mongrel called Shake, who looked like a long-haired fox. Shake was in Battersea for four months before he was re-homed in 1996. But he was brought back by his new owners because they said he was disobedient. Veronique did not find Shake disobedient. She would take him for walks in Battersea Park and he would behave perfectly, on or off the lead. And when she was busy, and the Volunteers came, they all wanted to walk Shake. He was such an easy-going dog, too: if the staff needed space for a dog, they knew they could put it in with Shake, because he got on with everybody.

None of the public, however, saw what everyone at Battersea saw in Shake. He stayed there all through 1997 and for the first part of 1998, adorable and affectionate, but unsold. And then, last March, Veronique was going on holiday and she began to worry: she had been walking Shake virtually every day and she was concerned he would miss her.

Amazingly, the day before she was due to leave for her break, Shake was bought. It was a relief for Veronique, but every time she went to say goodbye, she burst into tears.

'They were tears of happiness for Shake, as well as sadness for myself,' said Veronique. 'I was hoping he would get sold, but after so long, I did not have much hope. At lunchtime, I went to a pub with a colleague, Lisa, to toast Shake's future. By coincidence, he was leaving at the same time and he saw me and kept turning round, looking worried, as if he was thinking: "Where are you going? Why aren't you coming with me?" I watched him go and

DIET TIPS

Find out the weight of your dog. Your vet can weigh her, or you can take her onto the bathroom scales with you, and subtract your own weight.

Feed your dog according to weight, as instructed by text books and food manufacturers.

Feed a 'balanced diet' as indicated on leading brands of dog food.

Be very careful not to over-feed. Go easy on treats.

Chocolate can be poisonous to dogs.

Always have a clean bowl of water available for your dog.

Use a bowl size appropriate to the size of your dog. You will be tempted to fill an oversized bowl.

If your dog becomes obese, ask your vet about low-fat food.

Always use a clean feeding bowl.

A DOG FROM BATTERSEA

If you want to buy a dog from Battersea you will start by filling in a form. Some of the questions you will be asked are:

Have you owned a dog before? What type was it? How long did you have it? Where did it come from?

Do you have any other pets at home?

Why do you want a dog?

How near is an open space where you can exercise the dog?

Where will you let your dog go to toilet? How secure is that area?

Where will your dog stay during the day? At night? When you are away?

How long would a dog be left on its own? And, why?

Do you know the name of a veterinary surgeon?

Do you know the cost of vaccinating, neutering and feeding a dog?

Are you prepared for staff to visit your home?

then I went into the pub and howled. If ever a creature touched my heart, Shake did.'

Highbury was a plain-looking black and tan mongrel, about seven years old, who was gifted to Battersea by an owner June Haynes did not take to at all. He kept joking about how he could not keep the dog because it kept jumping over the fence and the neighbours were complaining. June could not see the funny side of a dog being given away for a reason like that.

Highbury was at Battersea for six months. It was not a happy stay. No one showed any interest in buying him – and, as a long-stayer, Highbury was often sharing his kennel with other dogs, who regularly beat him up. Then, one morning, the man who had given Highbury to Battersea turned up at the Home, wanting to know if the dog was still there. If he was, he wanted him back.

'The man must have felt guilty because he had saved up to put in some high fencing so that Highbury couldn't get out,' said June. 'It was lovely to see the dog so pleased to see his owner, but I did feel sorry for him. He must have wondered what was happening. It was as if he had served a six-month prison sentence when he had done nothing to deserve it. The owner had to pay for Highbury as though he were buying a dog. I think he got away lightly.'

When Sasha, a Collie-Shepherd cross, came in, she was a bag of bones. She was pitifully nervous, too, and as people walked past her kennel, she would hide behind her bed. If a kennel hand moved it, she would crawl away and cower in a corner, shaking: she did not want contact with anyone. And then Alex Martin came into her life.

Sasha heard something in Alex's voice she liked. She did not respond the first time, but gave a brief flicker of a wag the second. Alex was drawn to the dog and kept going back, trying to coax her out of her hideaway. Over the next two days, he would sit on her bed, an arm draped over it, stroking her gently. On the third day, he went to the kennel door and called: 'Sasha. Come on.' The dog leapt from behind the bed and jumped up at the bars, howling excitedly. Alex had won her confidence. He took her for walks in Battersea Park to socialize her, and they began to bond.

Eventually, a prospective buyer showed an interest in Sasha and Alex took her to the new land for an introduction. It took an hour for Sasha to leave Alex's side, but she finally responded to the man and he arranged to come back late that afternoon with his girlfriend. They both loved the dog, but Alex insisted they talk it over and come back another day.

'I was actually thinking of Sasha, not them,' Alex admitted. 'It was important to see her reaction when she saw them again. Fortunately, she took to them when they returned and I was able to let her go immediately. I was particularly thrilled because I feared that if she stayed with us too long she might lose her confidence and revert to how she was.

'Her new owners invited me round to see Sasha several months later. She looked at me and wagged her tail, but I could tell she wasn't sure who I was. I had a cup of tea with the couple and Sasha sat at her new owner's feet all the time. I was pleased. I was her past. He – and his partner – were her future.

'That's what re-homing is all about.'

CHAPTER NINE

Reunion for old friends

What would Mary Tealby have made of it?

When she started the Dog's Home in that tiny North London side street, all she wanted was to put food in the poor dogs' mouths and a roof over their heads. Now, nearly 140 years later, Battersea is caring for its animals, not just while they are in kennels waiting to be re-homed, but long after they have left Battersea. To Duncan Green and his staff, a Battersea dog is special and they have a responsibility to it. That is why Sue Oak, a computer programmer, was brought in 1993 to set up a Dog Register to log all known details of every dog brought in to the Home, and as much information as possible about who bought it. In other words, a complete record that would keep track of every dog that passed in and out of the Home.

In the past, staff had written everything about the new arrivals in long-hand in huge ledgers, and the transition to computers was not without its problems. But the old system was as antiquated as the old kennels under the arches and over the other side of the railway, now known by everyone at Battersea as the 'Unders and Overs'. If anyone wanted details of a dog or the statistics of particular types of dog over the previous year, it was a laborious process.

Happily the staff responded to Sue's training and, by the beginning of 1994, the new Dog Register was making life easier – and the job much quicker – for everyone, particularly those working in Customer Liaison who take the public's telephone enquiries. Now, all they had to do when anyone rang about a lost pedigree dog was carry out a search on the computer screen: if the dog was at Battersea, the computer would confirm it in less than a minute.

Sue Oak, Systems Administrator, helped by one of Battersea's Yorkies.

Today, there are about a dozen terminals around the home, all with access to information, and, not surprisingly,

all the staff now wonder how they had managed to cope before computers.

During the summer, Battersea opened its Lost Dogs' department, which provides a much-improved service to owners of lost dogs and cats by utilising a computer system provided by the now defunct National Strays Bureau, in addition to the Home's Dog Register. The new service is run from Whittington Lodge by a recent addition to the staff, Annie Mitchell, and Micky Swift.

Annie and Micky tour the kennels and cattery twice a day, in the hope that those animals who have been reported missing can be quickly reunited with owners who have contacted the department.

'It's all very exciting for us and is hugely beneficial to the public,' said Micky, who used to work with Jayne Payne, in Customer Liaison. 'Instead of people having to come to the Home every day, we can now take the details over the phone and do the searching for them. The new system also provides on-line information on police stations and vets in the owner's neighbourhood.'

Battersea is on the Internet, too: it has its own Website, enabling it to get across to a wider audience all that goes on at Battersea. The Website

Lost a dog? Jayne Payne (left) and Micky Swift are there to help reunite owners with their dogs. Micky has moved to the new Lost Dogs department, but she and Jayne are still a team.

OVERLEAF: Ali Taylor during one of her agility classes.

(www.dogshome.org), launched in Spring 1997 and up-dated in May this year, has many interesting features, including 'Pet on the Net', a fun page for the animals themselves. Owners send in photos of their pets, which are scanned into the page with as many personal details as they wish – including the animal's address for correspondence.

Every effort is made to find out as much as possible about every stray brought in, but no one knows for sure what has gone on in the animal's life, and why it has ended up in Battersea. The most diligent assessment, thorough Rehab, and all the tender loving care in the world can only go so far. The real test of how the animal is going to behave comes when it is in a new environment. That is when it can change dramatically and give its new owner problems.

That is why Battersea has set up the Behaviour Hotline – a telephone service that takes the heat out of new owners' anxieties by giving advice and comfort, no matter how long they have had the dog. Staff qualified to solve behaviour problems man the phone from 2.00 pm until 5.00 pm every weekday, and ask tried and tested questions to find out why the caller's dog is behaving in such a way. Then they send a programme of remedies that will, hopefully, cure it. If a dog is being destructive, for example, it will be important to define precisely *what* is being destroyed: Furniture? Clothing? Carpets? And where: near the front or back door? In only one room? If the animal is merely chewing, the Hotline helpers will want information such as: is the dog unhappy being left on its own? How long is it left? Does it follow the owner all over the house?

When the Hotline was started, these programmes were written out in long-hand for each owner, but 18 months ago, Katherine Hood, also a Volunteer, donated a computer and software to the Home to speed up the process.

Problems for most owners arise in the first week or two and are usually down to the dog's insecurity: it has spent weeks, maybe months, behind the bars of a kennel and simply can't cope. The dog is usually fine while the owners are in the house, but if it is left alone – even for half an hour – it misbehaves, either chewing on the furniture, or messing the floor, or whatever.

'Often much of the blame lies with the owner,' says Deputy Behaviourist, Ali Taylor. 'They take home a dog from Battersea and think: "Oh, my God, the poor thing's been ill-treated, we must spoil it to make it feel loved." That's understandable, but probably the worst thing to do. During that first week, they have probably spent all the time they can with the animal, then, the next week, maybe go back to work, expecting the dog to cope on its own. No wonder the dog freaks out and gets up to mischief. It's confused, bored, upset or frightened – or maybe all four!'

Before new owners leave Battersea with their dog, the re-homers explain how vital it is to lay down ground rules and get the dog into a routine. Sadly, most people are so excited and eager to get the new pet home that they do not listen. If they do, the advice doesn't always sink in.

'After all the interviewing and looking around, then hanging about while checks are made, they just want to get off home,' Ali said. 'The attitude mainly is: "We've had dogs before. We know what we're doing." Mine is: "You may have had dogs, but not rescue ones." And there's a huge difference.'

Dominance is a common problem: a dog that has been quiet and reserved in its kennel often becomes domineering once its confidence has been boosted in a home environment. Ali and her boss, Jackie Donaghy, have dealt with many cases where a dog becomes so dominant it feels it owns the owner – not the other way round!

Jackie said: 'A lot of people feel that if they don't show their dog love, they're neglecting it. In showing their love, however, they give the dog too many privileges and the animal gets its way so often it thinks: "This is brilliant. *I'm* in charge here. This person is under *my* control."

'People phone us, worried because their dog is lying just inside a room and won't allow them through the door, or it refuses to get off a settee and is challenging the owner to make it do so. This sort of behaviour – and others like it – needs to be curbed before it escalates and makes life unbearable for the owner. The last thing we want is for the dog to be brought back to Battersea because the owner is frightened, or the dog is unmanageable.

'The mistake most people make is thinking they have to be forceful – almost nasty – with their dog to make it obey commands. If a dog refuses to get off a settee, for instance, I've suggested offering it a treat and the owner has said: "It won't know it has done wrong if I do that." But I tell them that the dog will see it as a reward for doing what it has been told and will be more likely to get off the settee in future.'

The mistake many dog-owners make is rewarding their animal for behaviour that is not necessarily bad, but wrong.

'This merely re-reinforces that behaviour,' said Ali. 'How many times have you seen a dog get nervous walking past another dog – or in heavy, noisy traffic – and the owner pick it up and cuddle it, saying: "There, there, don't worry – nothing to be scared of – I'll give you a kiss." What they have done is

OVERLEAF: Saturday morning outside the Home. Prospective buyers and owners who have lost their pets wait for Battersea's doors to open.

make the dog think it has done the right thing. A better attitude would be to say: "Don't be silly. Get on with it," and, if possible, give the dog a squeaky toy to take its mind off its nervousness. I'm definitely in favour of owners teaching their dogs tricks. It's not cruel – it's fun. The dog gets stimulation and the owner gets to know the animal and understand it, which all makes for a better relationship.'

With this in mind, Ali has set up a training club at Battersea for people who have bought dogs from the Home. She gives agility classes and teaches traditional obedience commands – Sit, Stay, Heel, etc. – but in a different style. 'The accent is on fun,' she said. 'Fun for the dog and fun for the owner. Otherwise, it's pointless.'

Duncan Green was fortunate to take charge of this world-famous charity at a time when there were adequate funds to make generous and lasting improvements. The Committee believes that it is his bright, go-ahead style of leadership, combined with his competitive nature, that have helped to keep Battersea at the head of animal loving and caring organisations.

When a dog is up for sale, the re-homer has to meet *all* the prospective new owners.

Barely a week passes without a request from similar charities, both from the UK and from abroad, to view the Home. Battersea has become *the* place to visit. Quite recently, there have been visitors from America, Japan and South Africa. They were all impressed by what they saw.

'When I came here, I could see, as could the Committee, that we needed imaginative investment – in people, first of all, and in bricks and mortar; dedicated management and staff have helped me to achieve this. Battersea was one of the first rescue charities to microchip first dogs, then cats, and we have been innovative in re-homing and rehabilitation. Other charities are interested in our methods and I've shown hundreds of people round Kent Kennels; they all want to know the specific details about the building. Earlier this year, Peter Davis, the RSPCA's Director General, rang, asking if I'd mind showing two executives from a French animal charity round the Home.

'I'm happy to take people round. We're not in competition with other charities – we're in co-operation. I will help anyone, as long as that help is not detrimental to Battersea. If we have surplus equipment or beds, or whatever, and another charity has none, it's better if they have ours until they can afford their own. It does not matter where a dog is from, it still deserves something.'

Mind you, the former Army officer has been careful to keep his pride about the flushing loos to himself, after an embarrassing incident while showing them off to some visitors last year. Enthusing that the loos were his 'great contribution' to the Home, he bent down to pull the flush lever … and was horrified to see his glasses fall out of a top pocket and disappear down the loo, never to be seen again!

'That'll teach me to boast,' Duncan said, with a wry grin.

Something else Battersea is justifiably proud of is its low administrative costs. Last year it cost £4 million to run the Home, yet the administration bill was just 7.1 per cent of that – astonishingly low, compared with other charities. And the management team is just seven people, a small number in the charity business.

In the last ten years, more than £12 million has been spent on improvements, and more will be spent in the next few years. Battersea's immediate aim is to send the bulldozers into Unders and Overs and build new kennels on the new land at the rear of the Home. And since cats have now overtaken dogs as the nation's most popular pet, a new cattery is high on the agenda.

WHERE TO GET A DOG (IF YOU CAN'T GET ONE FROM THE DOGS' HOME BATTERSEA)

Contact your nearest rescue centre, (the RSPCA or look through yellow pages).

If you want to rescue a breed dog, contact the Kennel Club to obtain their breed rescue directory.

Ask your local vet if he, or she, knows of any local rescues, or puppies looking for homes.

Beware of answering advertisements in the papers. Always ask to see the mother or father of the puppy, and check the conditions.

Beware of getting a dog that might be from a puppy farm. You do not want to be supporting the puppy farm industry.

If you want to get a dog from a pet shop, check with the local vet first.

Amid a fun-filled carnival atmosphere, 'Old boys and girls' – from the biggest to the smallest – congregate in Battersea Park every summer with owners who share a common bond: a pride in having taken on a Battersea dog.

But re-homing remains the top priority. Plans are in hand for computers to be installed in the interview rooms in Kent Kennels, so that details of dogs – with photographs – can be brought up on the screen. This will make it easier and quicker to match dogs with suitable owners.

A huge drawback for people wanting to take on a Battersea dog are the costs they may face if the dog develops a medical condition. This is one of the reasons why Battersea is keen to introduce free vet treatment for every dog after it has been re-homed. At present, new owners are offered free after-sales veterinary treatment for three months, but hundreds more dogs would be re-homed if Battersea removed the long-term financial worry for prospective buyers.

Battersea wants to stay in touch with dogs they have re-homed, so a Grand Reunion for former residents is held every summer.

When Duncan thought of the idea, in June 1995, Nichola Vickers organized everything in just two months and achieved a resounding success: more than 600 'Old Boys and Girls' – from the biggest Great Dane to the tiniest Chihuahua – turned up in Battersea Park to renew acquaintances with friends made during their 'lost' years in the Home.

The event was such a success that more people were invited the following year and the turn-out of dogs rose to 800. Last year there were 1000 and in September this year the Reunion was more popular still. The day is simply a dog show with a walk – a fun day out, in a carefree carnival atmosphere, designed to thank those who have bought a Battersea dog, and to highlight the responsibilities of dog ownership. In the last two years, David Hamilton, the former BBC radio disc jockey, and Katie Boyle, have compered the 'Dandiest Dog', the 'Bonniest Bitch', and fancy dress competitions, and generally helped people get the best out of the day.

David was asked to serve on Battersea's committee after renewing a friendship with Katie, two years ago, at the Eukanuba 'Rescue Dog of the Year Show', which he was compering. He had become more and more interested in the dog world after he and his wife, Dreena, bought an adorable Labrador-Red Setter they named Rosie. David jumped at the chance to get involved with Battersea and, several months later, was formally invited to join the committee by its chairman, Lord Buchan. Since then, David has attended the monthly general committee meeting and, for the past year, has served on the publicity sub-Committee.

'I'm well aware that many of the committee know far more about dogs than me, but I've been listening hard and learned a lot,' said David, who also writes a column for *Dogs Monthly*.

Sadly, David had to miss out on this year's Reunion because he was committed to celebrating his sixtieth birthday with family and friends in Majorca. However such is his love of dogs, and Battersea in particular, that it did cross his mind to fly back for the event!

Shirley Piotrowski, who has organized the last three reunions, sees the event going on and on, attracting more and more dogs.

'Everyone has a lovely time, with fun the order of the day,' she said. 'One of my lasting memories is of hundreds of dogs diving into a 12ft square cake. Ali Taylor and I were patiently cutting it up into neat little pieces, but the dogs decided they couldn't wait that long. The reunions have proved so successful because all the people who come share one thing in common – a pride in being a Battersea dog owner. They've probably gone through some bad times, and are proud to show how their hard work has paid off. The day begins at 11.00 am and finishes around 5.00 pm with all the dogs being taken for a leisurely walk round the park.'

For many of the dogs, returning to the park where they were encouraged to put their difficulties behind them and learn to be social, is a happy, if strange, experience. For Duncan Green and his team, the sight of so many former residents showing no signs of the behaviour problems that worried everyone so much is enjoyable and intensely satisfying.

But for that brave woman who started the Dogs' Home Battersea in a stable yard, amid London's teeming, starving streets 138 years ago, the spectacle of more than 1000 once-unwanted and unhappy dogs together in harmony would be breath-taking. Such a wonderful celebration of well-fed, joyful dogs is surely the most fitting memorial of all for Mary Tealby.

Index